Young People's
First Aid

The St. John Ambulance
guide to basic first aid

St. John
Ambulance

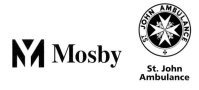

Young People's First Aid

Linda Allen RGN, St. John Ambulance
Edited by Andy Farquarson

First Edition 1997
ISBN 0 7234 3129 9

Author: Linda Allen RGN, St. John Ambulance
Publisher: Terry Robinson
Publisher's Editor: Andy Farquarson
Designer: Mark Howard
Photographer: Tim Fisher
Illustrator: Jenni Miller

Designed by Twenty-Five Educational,
25 Marylebone Road, London NW1 5JR

Printed in Barcelona by
Grafos S.A. Arte sobre papel, 1998

Foreword

From Her Royal Highness, the Princess Royal GCVO
Commandant-in-Chief, *(St. John Ambulance Cadets)*

BUCKINGHAM PALACE

No matter how young, everyone can save lives.

This book, written for the 10-15 year age group, is excellent reading, no matter how old you are. It presents the principles of first aid in a clear and easily understood way, and provides simple guidelines particularly suited to all youth organisations, not just our own St. John Ambulance Cadets with whom I am proud to be associated.

May I recommend this publication to you, and hope that if ever you find yourself in a situation where you need to use those skills learnt in practice, you do so with confidence and the knowledge that you can save lives!

Acknowledgements

THANKS
We wish to thank: the photographic
models from St. John Ambulance, Hall
School Wimbledon and Mosby;
Caroline Thomas for make-up; St. John
Ambulance London District and
St. John Supplies for props; Tim Fisher
for photography; and Mark Howard at
Twenty-Five Educational.

EDITORIAL INPUT
Sue Barrington; Peter Brown; Ann
Cable; Dr Andrew Catto; Ali Crane;
Dr Chris Lund; Graham Millward;
John Newman; Terry Perkins; Dr Tom
Rogerson; and Alan Sharkey.

Contents

An Introduction to First Aid

WHAT IS FIRST AID?

The term 'first aid' means the help someone gives to an ill or injured person before an ambulance, doctor or medically qualified person arrives.

'First aider' usually means someone who has taken a course in first aid and been awarded a certificate after passing an exam in the practical skills they have learnt. These certificates usually last three years but it is important that first aiders regularly practise their skills. Without practice, skills may be easily forgotten.

A first aider should aim to:

- preserve life (including their own);
- prevent the casualty's condition getting worse; and
- promote the casualty's recovery.

The person who is ill or injured is usually called a 'casualty' (that is the word we use throughout this book).

First aid learnt on a course or from a book is not the same as dealing with a real-life situation. Most of us feel scared when faced with 'the real thing' – even doctors and nurses feel like this sometimes. In some situations, you may be unsure whether you really want to help. You may be afraid of seeing blood or severe injuries, or feel that someone else would cope better than you.

You can only ever do your best. But sometimes, however hard you have tried, the casualty may not get better and may even die. In some cases even a doctor using all the facilities of a modern hospital cannot save a casualty's life. As long as you have tried your best, you should have no reason to feel guilty if a casualty does not recover.

Casualties need to feel safe. They will think they are in good hands if you:

- appear to be in control of yourself and the incident;
- act calmly;
- are gentle;
- talk kindly to the casualty; and
- do not leave them alone.

Explain to the casualty what you are doing. Answer questions as honestly as you can. If you do not know the answer, say so. Try not to separate a child from its mother, father, carer or other trusted person.

PROTECT YOURSELF

Giving first aid can sometimes be dangerous so always remember to protect yourself. Do not put yourself at risk by trying to do more than you possibly can. First aid is sometimes messy, smelly or simply 'yukkie'. You may worry that you won't be able to cope with a real situation but most first aiders come through with flying colours.

You may also worry about catching HIV (AIDS) or Hepatitis B. It is true that the viruses that cause these diseases are spread by blood-to-blood contact. However there are no known cases of either virus being passed through giving mouth-to-mouth resuscitation.

You should always remember the following points:
- Wash your hands thoroughly before and after giving first aid.
- Always wash off any splashed blood with soap and water as soon as possible (even though blood on undamaged skin should not be a problem).
- If you have any wounds or open sores, cover them with a waterproof dressing.
- Use disposable gloves when giving first aid, where possible.
- Be very careful not to prick yourself with any needle or cut yourself on broken glass.
- Wearing gloves, mop up any body fluids from the floor or other surfaces using bleach solution (two teaspoonfuls of bleach in each litre of water).
- Put any used dressings into yellow clinical waste bags, which should always be disposed of properly.
- Talk to your doctor about immunisation against Hepatitis B.

AFTER AN INCIDENT

Helping at an emergency can be stressful. Very often, you may get a 'delayed reaction'. You may feel upset, worried or guilty that you did not do enough. These feelings are normal. Don't keep your worries to yourself or try to cope on your own. Always talk to your friends, parents, youth leader or doctor about your feelings.

Emergency!

EMERGENCIES

An emergency is any dangerous incident that happens suddenly and needs quick action to remove or reduce the danger.

At an emergency, you may need to do several things at once. You may be the person who takes charge of (or 'manages') an incident. If so, keep calm!

Your first step should be to think for a moment about what you will need to do. Try to work to a plan, following the emergency action steps listed below.

MANAGING INCIDENTS

Assess the situation

Find out what has happened. Tell the people at the incident that you have had first aid training. Ask if anyone else can help.

Safety

Take action to prevent further danger. Ask yourself whether the casualty or anyone else (including yourself) is in danger. Do not put yourself at risk or try to do too much on your own.

Give emergency first aid

As soon as you are sure it is safe, find out what is wrong with the casualty. Use the ABC of Resuscitation (described in the next chapter) then, depending on what you find, give suitable first aid.

Get help

Call the emergency services by dialling 999 from any telephone (how to do this is described below). Get other people at the incident to help; for instance, by asking someone to phone for an ambulance.

After the incident

When the incident is over, you may need to clean the area, tidy up, restock your first aid kit, or look after friends and relatives of the casualty. Remember to look after yourself as well. If you have any worries, talk them over with your parents, friends or youth leader.

HOW TO TELEPHONE FOR HELP

You can call the emergency services from *any* telephone – a phonebox, payphone, private phone, mobile phone or motorway emergency phone. You do not need to have any money with you. Emergency calls are *free*.

In Britain, the emergency number is **999** but you can also get through using the international emergency number **112**.

All 999 calls are free.

The telephone operator will ask you which emergency service you want:
- police;
- ambulance;
- fire service;
- coastguard; or
- mine, mountain, cave and fell rescue.

Say which service you need. If there are casualties, ask for the ambulance service.

Be ready to tell the operator the telephone number you are calling from and your name.

If you are not sure exactly where you are, don't worry. Your call can be traced so never put the phone down until you are told to do so.

When the operator puts you through to the ambulance service control officer, you should be ready to tell them:
- The telephone number you are calling from.
- Where the incident is (tell them the road name and number if you can and details such as road junctions or other landmarks).
- The type of incident (for instance, it might be a road accident involving one car and two bicycles, with two casualties).
- Tell them anything you know about the casualties such as their age, their sex, and their condition and situation (for instance, a middle-aged lady driver with head injuries might be trapped in her car).
- Warn of any dangers such as fog, ice, leaking petrol, or a smell of gas (if there is a fire, the control officer will alert the fire service).

TYPES OF INCIDENT

SERIOUS ACCIDENTS

These include train crashes, pile-ups on motorways, gas explosions and so on. At a serious accident, you may be faced with a large number of casualties. ***Don't panic*** – remember, you will not be on your own.

It is important to let the emergency services know exactly what has happened. Then they can send as much help as possible – and the right sort of help. For instance, the accident may need special equipment or experts.

While you are waiting for the emergency services to arrive, make a quick assessment of the casualties. Give suitable first aid if you can but make sure it is safe to do so. ***Never put your own safety at risk.***

When the emergency services arrive, offer to help. However, you must leave the scene if they ask you to.

MULTIPLE CASUALTIES

At some incidents, there may be more than one casualty to deal with. You must decide who needs your help first – the DRABC drill described in the next chapter will help you decide. Anyone who is obviously dead should be left because your help will be of more use to living casualties. This is a hard decision to make but remember you may be able to save someone's life.

When the emergency services arrive, offer to help. However, you must leave the scene if they ask you to.

You should treat the casualties in the following order:
> **First** – unconscious casualties and those with life-threatening conditions.
> **Second** – casualties with serious injuries such as severe bleeding, burns, and so on.
> **Third** – less seriously injured casualties.

ROAD ACCIDENTS

A road accident could be anything from someone falling off a bicycle to a major motorway crash with many casualties. Usually there will be dangers at the scene, such as oncoming traffic, so you must make the area as safe as possible. To protect yourself, the casualties and other road users, remember the following points:

- Never run across a busy road without first checking for oncoming traffic.
- Ask bystanders to stop the traffic.
- Get someone to set up warning triangles or lights at least 200 metres away in each direction (many cars carry a warning triangle in the boot, used to give advance warning to approaching traffic).
- If cars are involved in a crash, put the handbrakes on and switch off the engines by turning the ignition key.
- Make sure nobody smokes because cigarettes, lighters or matches might start a fire.

Always turn off the car's ignition, whether the engine is running or not.

Unconscious casualties at road accidents

If an unconscious casualty at a road accident needs to be taken out of a car, you should have at least three people to help you. One helper should support the casualty's shoulders, one helper the hips and abdomen and one the legs. You should support the casualty's head and control all the movements. But *do not* move a casualty unless it is absolutely necessary. You should always treat unconscious casualties with the same care as you would if they had a neck injury (dealing with neck injuries is described on page 130, chapter **11**).

Poisonous substances   Flammable substances

Radioactive substances   Corrosive substances

Dangerous substances

Sometimes, vehicles involved in a road accident may be carrying dangerous substances. These vehicles may have a 'Hazchem' placard displayed on them to warn about possible dangers.

If you think there may be a risk from dangerous substances or toxic gases, *do not* attempt to rescue the casualties unless you are *sure it is safe*.

Stay upwind of the accident so that any fumes are blown away from you and keep bystanders back as well. Make a note of the information on the 'Hazchem' sign to pass onto the emergency services.

FIRES

Fires can spread very quickly so warn anyone at risk. Call the emergency services as soon as possible. Do your best to help everyone out of the building. As you leave, shut doors behind you to slow down the spread of the fire.

You *must never*:
- put yourself at risk;
- use the lift in a building if there is a fire;
- go into a burning or smoke-filled building; or
- open a door leading to a fire.

Close doors on a fire, activate fire alarms and leave the building quickly but calmly.

If you are trapped in a burning building:
- go into a room with a window and shut the door;
- put a blanket or coat along the bottom of the door to keep out the smoke; and
- open the window and shout for help.

Clothing on fire
Always remember the 'Stop, Drop And Roll' drill.

Stop the casualty from running around and panicking.
Drop the casualty onto the ground.
Wrap the casualty in a coat, a blanket (but *not* a nylon or cellular one), a rug or some heavy material.
Roll the casualty along the ground to put out the flames.

Use material such as a coat or rug to smother the flames.

If water is available, use it to put out the flames.
    If your own clothes catch fire, wrap yourself up in suitable material and roll along the ground.

ELECTRICAL INJURIES

High voltage current

If someone comes into contact with high voltage current (such as that in power lines, railway lines and overhead cables) they will usually be killed immediately.

You must not go near any casualties until you have been *officially told* the power has been cut off. Until you are told, keep at least 20 metres away from the casualty because high voltage electricity can jump through the air (this is called 'arcing').

How you can help

- Call the emergency services immediately.
- Keep bystanders well away.
- When you have been told it is *safe to do so*, assess the casualty following the DRABC drill.
- Treat any injuries as necessary.

Handy hint!

Keep at least 20 metres away from the casualty because high voltage electricity can jump through the air.

Low voltage current

The low voltage current that is supplied to our homes can injure people and sometimes kill them. People can come into contact with the current through faulty switches, frayed wires or by using damaged or unsafe electrical appliances. Never touch a casualty until the current is switched off or they are not in contact with it. Never touch an electrical appliance or wiring with wet hands.

Never use anything metallic – a wooden broom will protect you from harm. Find insulating material, such as a telephone directory, to stand on.

How you can help
- Switch the current off at the mains.
- If you can't switch off at the mains, switch the current off at the wall socket or pull out the plug.
- Call the emergency services.
- When you are **sure** the current has been switched off, assess the casualty following the DRABC drill.
- Resuscitate the casualty if necessary.
- Cool any burns with plenty of cold water.

DROWNING

Water is fascinating but it can be dangerous. Young children are particularly at risk. As a first aider, you may come across drowning incidents at the seaside, rivers, reservoirs, canals, docks, lakes, ponds, and garden pools.

Rescuing casualties
Sometimes you may have to rescue someone from the water who is drowning (or appears to have drowned).

Trained lifesavers are taught never to put themselves at risk. So unless you are a good swimmer and absolutely **sure it is safe** to do so, **never go into the water** yourself.

Instead of getting into the water, **reach out** to the casualty, using your hand, a stick, a pole, a fishing rod, a branch, or something else suitable.

Handy hint!

If you do have to go into the water, it is much safer to wade than swim.

There may be rescue equipment, such as a rope, a float or a lifebuoy, which you can *throw* to the casualty. If not, you may be able to throw something else that floats such as a plastic drink bottle, a plastic football or a beach ball. You may be able to make a 'rope' to throw by tying together items of clothing such as ties, scarves, sweaters or coats.

Remember *reach or throw, don't go!*

Make sure the airway is clear.

How you can help at a drowning incident

- Keep the casualty's head lower than the rest of their body to help stop vomiting and let any water drain away.
- Assess the casualty, following the DRABC drill (but *don't* waste time trying to get water out of the casualty's lungs).
- Call the emergency services.
- Resuscitate the casualty if necessary.
- Wrap the casualty against the cold and treat them for hypothermia if necessary (hypothermia is described in chapter 10).
- Make sure the casualty goes to hospital, even if they seem to have fully recovered.

Initial assessment and the ABC of Resuscitation

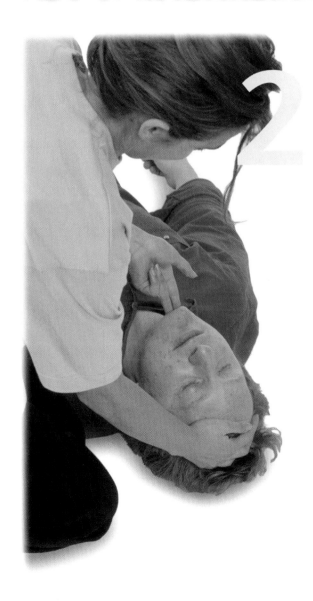

Initial assessment – DRABC

Once you are sure the area is safe, you can start to help sick or injured casualties. Although there may be obvious injuries, such as a broken leg, your first step is to check for any life-threatening problems by following the resuscitation sequence.

The sequence is easy to remember by its initial letters – **DRABC** (think of *Doctor ABC*):

Danger
Response
Airway
Breathing
Circulation

Once you are sure there is no *danger*, check the casualty's *response*. Decide whether the casualty is unconscious because an unconscious casualty needs immediate emergency aid. If you think there might be head or neck injuries, only move the casualty if you have to.

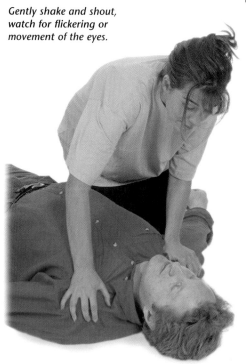

Gently shake and shout, watch for flickering or movement of the eyes.

HOW TO CHECK RESPONSE
Gently shake the casualty's shoulders but be careful not to move their head or neck.
Call the casualty's name (if you know it) or give a command such as 'Open your eyes'.
If the casualty is conscious, is breathing and has a pulse, give suitable first aid treatment and get help.
If there is *no response*, the casualty is unconscious and you should follow the ABC of Resuscitation.

THE ABC OF RESUSCITATION

Remember the letters **ABC**:
Airway
Breathing
Circulation

AIRWAY

Unless their airway is clear, a casualty cannot breathe. When someone is unconscious, their tongue may fall to the back of their throat and block their airway.

To open a casualty's airway, put two fingers under the point of their chin.

Put your other hand on their forehead. At the same time, lift the casualty's jaw and tilt their head back slightly.

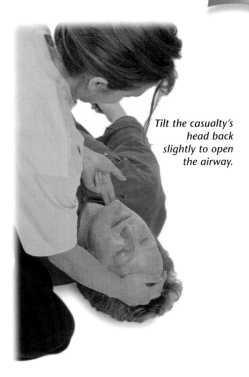

Tilt the casualty's head back slightly to open the airway.

BREATHING

When you have opened the casualty's airway, check their breathing. You must keep the airway open while you check.

Look, listen and feel to check the casualty's breathing.

* **Look** to see if their chest is moving up and down.

Look along the chest for any movement.

- **Listen** for sounds of breathing by putting your ear close to the casualty's mouth.
- **Feel** for their breath against your cheek.

Check for up to *ten seconds* before you decide whether the casualty is breathing or not.

CIRCULATION

Circulation means that the heart is pumping blood round the body. The beating of the heart can be felt as 'the pulse' at certain places on the body.

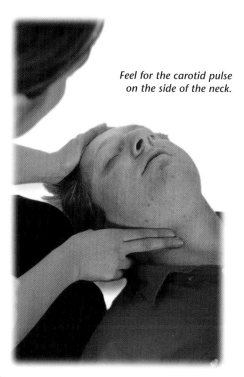

Feel for the carotid pulse on the side of the neck.

Here's how to check the casualty's pulse.

- Find the casualty's pulse in the hollow on the side of their neck beside their voice box (this is called the 'carotid' pulse).
- Feel the pulse on the side of the casualty's neck which is nearest to you by pressing your finger tips gently on the artery (*do not* use your thumb).

Check for up to *ten seconds* before you decide whether the casualty's heart is beating or not.

THE RESUSCITATION SEQUENCE – ACTING ON YOUR ABC FINDINGS

Once you have opened the casualty's airway and checked their breathing and circulation, you should give emergency aid. This may mean giving cardiopulmonary resuscitation (called CPR for short).

CPR means giving mouth-to-mouth ventilations and chest compressions together. How to give CPR is described in the next chapter.

What you will need to do depends on what you find. For instance, the casualty may be conscious or unconscious, they may be breathing or not breathing, and they may or not have a pulse.

The resuscitation sequence is summarised in the diagram on page 16.

THE RESUSCITATION SEQUENCE

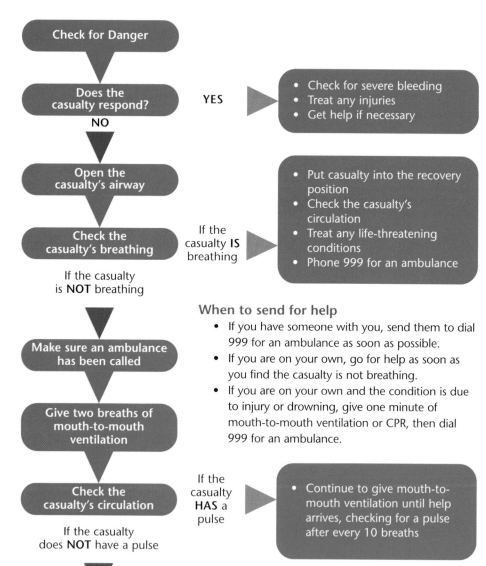

Check for Danger

Does the casualty respond?   **YES**
NO

- Check for severe bleeding
- Treat any injuries
- Get help if necessary

Open the casualty's airway

Check the casualty's breathing   If the casualty **IS** breathing

- Put casualty into the recovery position
- Check the casualty's circulation
- Treat any life-threatening conditions
- Phone 999 for an ambulance

If the casualty is **NOT** breathing

Make sure an ambulance has been called

Give two breaths of mouth-to-mouth ventilation

When to send for help

- If you have someone with you, send them to dial 999 for an ambulance as soon as possible.
- If you are on your own, go for help as soon as you find the casualty is not breathing.
- If you are on your own and the condition is due to injury or drowning, give one minute of mouth-to-mouth ventilation or CPR, then dial 999 for an ambulance.

Check the casualty's circulation   If the casualty **HAS** a pulse

- Continue to give mouth-to-mouth ventilation until help arrives, checking for a pulse after every 10 breaths

If the casualty does **NOT** have a pulse

Give CPR until help arrives

How to give CPR

3

In the last chapter, we learned about the ABC of Resuscitation (Airway, Breathing and Circulation). We looked at the **resuscitation sequence** as part of the initial assessment of a patient. Now we will take a closer look at cardiopulmonary resuscitation itself.

Our bodies need oxygen to survive. Enough oxygen must reach the vital organs, especially the heart and brain, for life to continue. If the brain is not receiving enough oxygen, within three to four minutes it will stop working properly, the casualty will lose consciousness, breathing and the heart will stop and the casualty will die.

There are three main areas which will affect the oxygen reaching the brain – airway, breathing and circulation.

> **Airway** – Air which contains oxygen is breathed in through the nose and mouth, and passes down the windpipe (trachea) into the lungs. This passageway may be blocked by food, vomit, blood or by the tongue falling back and relaxing if a casualty is unconscious.
>
> **Breathing** – When air reaches the lungs, oxygen passes into the blood supply. If breathing does not take place, this exchange will not happen, and there will not be enough oxygen in the blood.
>
> **Circulation** – Once oxygen has entered the blood supply, it is pumped around the body by the heart. If the heart has stopped or is not working properly, oxygen will not reach the brain and other vital organs.

RESUSCITATION

Resuscitation means trying to revive a casualty who is not breathing, or who has no pulse, or who appears to be dead. The aim of resuscitation is to keep oxygen circulating round the casualty's body until an ambulance, a doctor or other medically qualified helper arrives.

If a casualty has stopped breathing or their heart has stopped, a first aider must make every effort to get oxygen into the lungs and make sure the blood circulates, carrying the oxygen to the organs. To do this, the first aider must be able to give cardiopulmonary resuscitation (called CPR for short). Cardiopulmonary is made up of two medical words: cardio means to do with the heart and pulmonary means to do with the lungs. To get the oxygen into a casualty's lungs, a first aider uses a method called mouth-to-mouth ventilation (you may have heard this called 'the kiss of life' or 'rescue breathing'). To make sure the oxygen is carried round the body, the first aider uses a method called chest compressions. CPR is when these two actions are done together.

By itself, CPR is not usually enough to completely revive a patient. That may require special medical equipment such as a defibrillator (a device to re-start the heart). But CPR is vital to 'buy time' before specialist help arrives. If you know how to give CPR, *your actions can save lives*.

A casualty has a better chance of surviving if:
- enough oxygen is supplied to the brain by CPR;
- a defibrillator is quickly used to restart the heart; and
- the casualty gets to expert help and care in hospital as soon as possible.

This is called the **'chain of survival'**. If any of the links in the chain are too slow or are missing, the casualty's chance of surviving will be reduced.

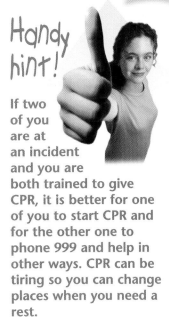

Handy hint!

If two of you are at an incident and you are both trained to give CPR, it is better for one of you to start CPR and for the other one to phone 999 and help in other ways. CPR can be tiring so you can change places when you need a rest.

Early Access Get help as soon as possible. If someone else is there, tell them to phone 999 for an ambulance but make sure they have the right information to pass on.

Early CPR Start cardiopulmonary resuscitation (CPR) as soon as possible.

Early Defibrillation Use a defibrillator to re-start the heart as soon as possible.

Early Advanced Care Get the casualty to expert care as soon as possible.

MOUTH-TO-MOUTH VENTILATION

Even when your body has taken its share of oxygen, the air you breathe out still contains enough oxygen to keep a casualty alive. In fact, the atmosphere contains about 21 per cent oxygen and the air you breathe out about 16 per cent.

So you can use the air you breathe out to supply oxygen to a casualty by gently blowing into their lungs. This will keep up the level of oxygen in the casualty's blood. If the casualty's heart has stopped, you will also have to give chest compressions to make sure the blood circulates round their body carrying the oxygen to their vital organs.

Handy hint!

If mouth injuries mean you cannot make a good seal, you may need to give mouth-to-nose ventilation. Open the casualty's mouth to let the breath out.

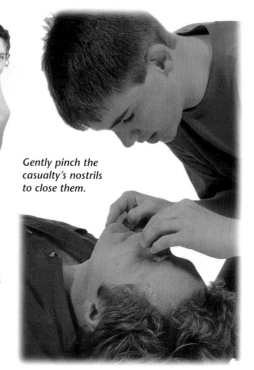

Gently pinch the casualty's nostrils to close them.

How to give mouth-to-mouth ventilations

1   The casualty should be laying flat on their back.
2   Remove any obvious obstruction from the casualty's mouth (this might be bits of food or broken teeth) but leave false teeth in place if they are not loose.
3   Open the casualty's airway by tilting their head and lifting their chin.
4   Gently pinch the casualty's nostrils together using your first finger and thumb.
5   Take a deep breath and put your lips around the casualty's mouth. Make a good seal with your lips then blow steadily into the casualty's mouth until you see their chest rise. Take about two seconds for the full 'breath'.
6   Take your mouth away and let the casualty's chest sink right back down, which will take about four seconds.
7   Repeat steps 4-6.
8   If the casualty's chest does not rise during the ventilations, check:
    • their airway is open;
    • you have a good seal round their mouth;
    • you have closed their nose completely; and
    • their airway is not blocked by vomit or a foreign object, such as a sweet.
9   If the casualty's chest still won't rise after you have checked these things, check their mouth again for any obvious obstruction and remove it if you can.

10 Try three more breaths of mouth-to-mouth ventilation. If the casualty's chest still won't rise, check the points in step 8 again.
11 If the casualty's chest still won't rise after checking the points in step 8 again, check for circulation and start the treatment for an unconscious choking casualty (described in chapter 5).

Mouth-to-stoma ventilation

Sometimes, you may have to resuscitate a casualty who has a permanent opening in the front of the neck through which they breathe. This opening is called a stoma.

If the casualty has a stoma, you will have to put your mouth over it and give mouth-to-stoma ventilation. If the casualty's chest does not rise and air escapes from their mouth, the casualty may be a 'partial neck breather'. If this happens, you should close their mouth and nose with your thumb and fingers as you breathe into their stoma.

CHEST COMPRESSIONS AND CPR

This section deals with giving chest compressions to an **adult** casualty. Resuscitation for **children** is described later in this chapter.

If you find that a casualty has no pulse, it means their heart has stopped. As a first aider you must give them chest compressions as soon as possible to keep their blood circulating, particularly to their brain. The blood must contain oxygen so chest compressions are always given together with mouth-to-mouth ventilation. Giving the two together, as we have seen, is called CPR.

Use two fingers to find the point where the ribs meet.

How to give chest compressions

1 Find the place where the casualty's lower ribs meet the breastbone and lay two of your fingers on their breastbone at that point.

2   Put the heel of your other hand on their breastbone, just above where your two fingers are.

3   Now put your other hand on top of the first one and lock your fingers together.

4   Position yourself so your shoulders are directly above the centre of the casualty's chest. Keep your arms straight and press down on their chest, pushing it down about four or five centimetres.

5   Let off the pressure but keep your hands in position.

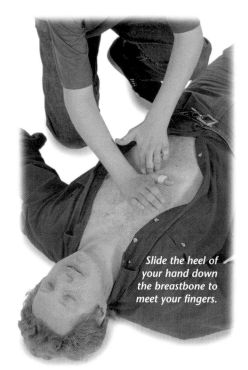

Slide the heel of your hand down the breastbone to meet your fingers.

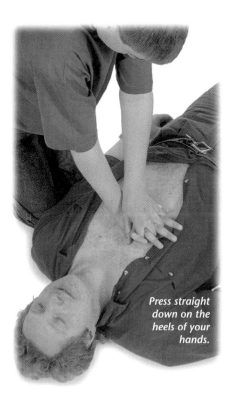

Press straight down on the heels of your hands.

6   Repeat the compression 15 times, at the rate of 100 compressions each minute (that's very roughly three compressions every two seconds).

7   Now give two breaths of mouth-to-mouth ventilation.

8   Carry on with CPR, following the sequence of **15 compressions to 2 breaths** until help arrives.

9   If the casualty's colour changes from white or blue-ish to pink, you should stop to check their pulse. Otherwise don't stop to do so. If you find the casualty now has a pulse, stop compressions but carry on with mouth-to-mouth ventilations if necessary.

GIVING CPR TO CHILDREN
So far, we have looked at CPR for adult casualties. There are differences in the way you should give CPR to child and baby casualties. There are also slight differences between the methods used with children and babies.

What exactly do we mean by 'baby', 'child' and 'adult' when we are talking about CPR? A baby is an infant who is less than one year old. A child is aged between one and seven years. Anyone aged eight years and over should be treated as an adult for CPR.

It is rare for the heart to stop in younger children or babies, but they are more likely to have problems with their breathing. Firstly, remember **DRABC** just as you would with an adult casualty.

Danger
- Make sure it is safe to go to the casualty.
Response
- Talk to the casualty and gently shake their shoulders. For babies, pick them up and shake them *gently* but be sure to support their head as you do so.
- If the casualty is conscious and breathing, treat them and get help as needed.
- If there is no response, you must follow the ABC of Resuscitation
Airway
- Put the baby or child onto a firm surface.
- Open their airway by putting your hand on their forehead and gently lifting their chin.

Handy hint!

If you are giving first aid to a baby or toddler, don't forget their mum and dad. Often mum will want to keep holding her baby. You can suggest she puts the baby on a table and holds its hand while you give the CPR. Instead of putting a young baby in the recovery position, let mum hold the baby face-down in her arms or on her lap.

Breathing
- Put your ear close to the casualty's mouth.
- Look to see if their chest is rising and falling.
- Listen for sounds of breathing.
- Feel for breath on your cheek.
- If the casualty is breathing, place them in the recovery position.
- If they are *not* breathing, give five breaths of mouth-to-mouth ventilations, then check their circulation.

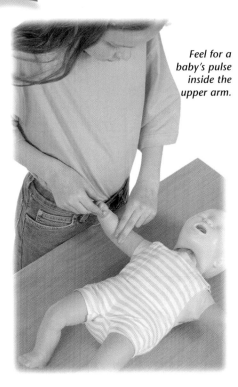

Feel for a baby's pulse inside the upper arm.

Circulation

Check the casualty's pulse for up to ten seconds.

- If the casualty is a baby, check the pulse inside their upper arm by lightly pressing two fingers onto the bone.
- If the casualty is a child, check the pulse in their neck by lightly pressing two fingers to one side of the neck.

Feel for a child's carotid pulse on the side of the neck.

Handy hint!

If the casualty is big enough so that you have to move from their chest to reach their head when you give mouth-to-mouth ventilations, you should use the adult method of CPR.

THE RESUSCITATION SEQUENCE FOR CHILDREN AND BABIES

Once you have cleared the casualty's airway and checked their breathing and circulation, you should give emergency aid. As with an adult casualty, what you will need to do depends on what you find.

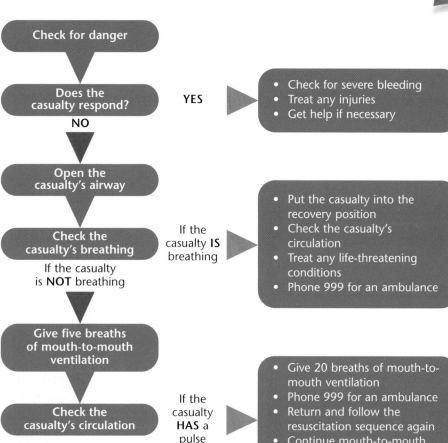

Check for danger

Does the casualty respond?   **YES**

- Check for severe bleeding
- Treat any injuries
- Get help if necessary

NO

Open the casualty's airway

Check the casualty's breathing

If the casualty **IS** breathing

- Put the casualty into the recovery position
- Check the casualty's circulation
- Treat any life-threatening conditions
- Phone 999 for an ambulance

If the casualty is **NOT** breathing

Give five breaths of mouth-to-mouth ventilation

Check the casualty's circulation

If the casualty **HAS** a pulse

- Give 20 breaths of mouth-to-mouth ventilation
- Phone 999 for an ambulance
- Return and follow the resuscitation sequence again
- Continue mouth-to-mouth ventilation, checking for a pulse after every 20 breaths

If the casualty does **NOT** have a pulse (or under 60 beats per minute in a baby)

- Give one minute of CPR
- Phone 999 for an ambulance
- Return and follow the resuscitation sequence again
- Continue giving CPR until help arrives

When to send for help

- If you have someone with you, send them to dial 999 for an ambulance as soon as possible.
- If you are on your own, give one minute of mouth-to-mouth ventilation or CPR, then phone 999 for an ambulance, taking the baby or child with you if possible.

How to give mouth-to-mouth (or mouth-to-nose) ventilation to babies and children

Look inside the casualty's mouth for any obstruction that can be easily removed.

Never touch the back of a baby or young child's throat with your fingers. The area is very soft and may swell and bleed if you touch it. This might block their airway.

Clear the casualty's airway.

If the casualty is a baby under one year old:
1   Put your lips around the baby's mouth and nose.

Lift the chin and tilt the head to clear the airway.

Pinch the nostrils to close them.

2   Breathe gently into their lungs until you see their chest rise.
3   As their chest rises, stop blowing and let the chest sink back down again.
4   Repeat the breaths, at a rate of about 20 breaths each minute.

If the casualty is a child between one and seven years old:
1   Put your lips around the child's mouth while gently pinching their nostrils closed.

2   Breathe gently into their lungs until you see their chest rise.
3   As their chest rises, stop blowing and let their chest to sink back down again.
4   Repeat the breaths allowing about two seconds for each full breath. Aim at a rate of about 20 breaths each minute.

How to give chest compressions to babies under one year old
If you find that a baby or child has no pulse, it means their heart has stopped (just as it does in an adult casualty). As a first aider you must give them chest compressions as soon as possible to keep their blood circulating, with mouth-to-mouth (or mouth-to-nose) ventilations to provide the vital oxygen.

If a baby's heart rate drops below one beat each second, their circulation will not be effective and you must start chest compressions to help keep the blood moving. This only applies to babies – never give chest compressions to older children or adults if they have a pulse.

1   Lay the baby down on their back on a firm surface.
2   Put two fingers on the baby's lower breastbone. The correct spot is a finger's width below an imaginary line joining the baby's nipples. Using just the tips of your fingers, press the baby's chest down by one third of its depth.
3   Repeat five times at a rate of 100 compressions each minute.
4   Give one mouth-to-mouth (or mouth-to-nose) ventilation.
5   Continue the sequence of five compressions to one ventilation for one minute.
6   Carry the baby to a telephone and phone 999 for an ambulance.
7   Continue CPR, giving five compressions to one ventilation, until help arrives.

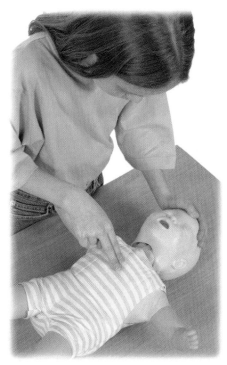

Only use two fingers for chest compressions.

How to give chest compressions to children between one and seven years old

1   Lay the child down on their back on a firm surface.
2   Put two fingers of one hand on the place on their chest where their lower ribs meet the end of their breastbone.
3   Place the heel of your other hand on their breastbone just above your two fingers.
4   Use the heel of **one hand only** to press the child's chest down by one-third of its depth.
5   Repeat five times at a rate of 100 compressions each minute.
6   Give one mouth-to-mouth ventilation.

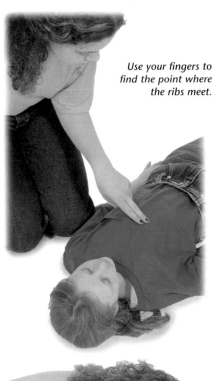

Use your fingers to find the point where the ribs meet.

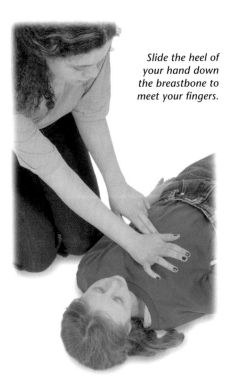

Slide the heel of your hand down the breastbone to meet your fingers.

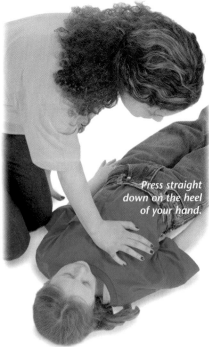

Press straight down on the heel of your hand.

7   Continue the sequence of five compressions to one ventilation for one minute.
8   If the child is small enough, carry them with you to a telephone, and phone 999 for an ambulance.
9   If you have had to leave the casualty to phone for an ambulance, when you return follow the resuscitation sequence again and act on what you find.
10 Continue CPR, giving five compressions to one ventilation, until help arrives.

THE RECOVERY POSITION

If they have no other life-threatening condition, unconscious casualties who are breathing and have a pulse should always be put in the **recovery position**.

The recovery position stops the casualty's tongue from falling back and blocking their airway. It also lets liquids (such as vomit) drain out of the casualty's mouth – this stops the liquids getting into their airway and blocking it.

Take off the casualty's glasses (spectacles) if they are wearing any. Take any bulky things out of their pockets before you put the casualty in the recovery position.

HOW TO PUT A CASUALTY IN THE RECOVERY POSITION
1   Make sure the casualty's airway is open.
2   Straighten their legs. Move their arm nearest to you out at right angles, with the elbow bent, and the palm facing upwards.

Handy hint!

When you put a casualty in the recovery position, you may need to alter the sequence and position slightly, depending on the casualty's injuries and the position you found them in.

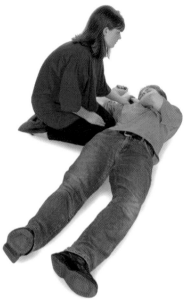

3   Bring the casualty's other arm across their chest and hold their hand against their cheek with their palm facing outward.

4   With your other hand, get hold of the outside of the thigh furthest away from you. Pull their knee up, keeping their foot flat on the ground.

5   Keeping their hand pressed against their cheek, roll the casualty towards you. Use your knees to support them and stop them from turning too far forwards.

6   Tilt their head back to keep the airway open, adjusting their hand under their cheek if necessary.

7   Move their upper leg so that hip and knee are at right angles.

8   When the casualty is in the recovery position, check their breathing and pulse regularly while you wait for help to arrive.

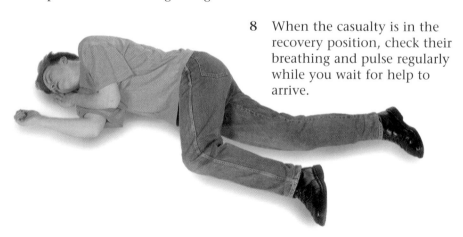

Diagnosis

4

When you have made the initial assessment and followed the resuscitation sequence, you can begin to treat the illness or injury. In most cases, you will be helping a conscious casualty who does not have a life-threatening problem.

But you still need to find out what is wrong with the casualty so that you can give the correct treatment.

Finding out what is wrong with the casualty is called **making a diagnosis**. The diagnosis is based on the casualty's **history, signs** and **symptoms**.

HISTORY

When you arrive at an incident, you may be able to see what has happened. For instance, the casualty may have fallen off a bicycle. You should ask the casualty and anyone else who saw the incident exactly what happened.

Questions to ask might include:
- What was the casualty doing at the time?
- What were the conditions like (for instance, was it raining or was the casualty in a hot and stuffy room)?
- What is the casualty's name and address?
- How old is the casualty?
- Does the casualty have any illness or take any medication?

SIGNS AND SYMPTOMS

A **sign** is something *you* can see, feel, hear, touch or smell. Signs include things like bleeding, sweating, swelling, noisy breathing, and the smell of alcohol.

A **symptom** is something *the casualty* feels, sees, hears, or smells.

Symptoms include things like aches and pains, dizziness, and feeling very cold, hot or thirsty.

Use your senses to help you make a diagnosis – look, listen, feel and smell.

Looking

At the scene:
- Notice the surroundings.
- Look for any containers such as bottles of tablets, alcohol, syringes, aerosols.

With the casualty:
- Watch the casualty's breathing.
- Look for bleeding, colour of skin, sweating, swelling, bruising, embedded objects, vomit, and needle marks on the arms.

- Notice the expression on the casualty's face.
- Look for legs or arms bent at funny angles.
- Look for the response to touch or your voice.

If the casualty is unconscious, look for clues such as special medical information bracelets, hospital cards and sugar.

Listening
Listen to the casualty. Ask them what has happened. Ask about pain, drowsiness, loss of consciousness, loss of movement or sensation, dizziness or sickness. Ask if they feel thirsty, hot or cold.

Listen to bystanders. Again, ask what has happened and how. Ask if anyone else has been involved.

If the casualty is unconscious, listen for breathing sounds.

Feeling
Examine the casualty and carry out a 'top to toe survey'. Feel for:
- Dampness, swelling, deformity, or tenderness.
- The casualty's temperature and pulse.
- Anything unusual.

Smelling
At the scene:
- Is there a smell of gas or fumes, burning, solvents or glue?

With the casualty:
- Does the casualty's breath smell of alcohol, solvents or acetone?
- Is there a smell caused by incontinence?

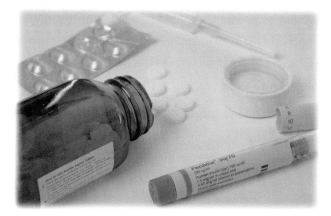

Look for any containers such as bottles of tablets, alcohol, syringes, aerosols.

THE 'TOP TO TOE SURVEY'

When you have taken any immediate action that is needed, examine your casualty carefully. Start at the head and work down. You may need to move or remove clothing, but try not to move the casualty more than is necessary. Try to conduct the examination in the position the casualty was found in. Use both hands, and always compare one side of the casualty with the other to help you find swelling and deformity more easily.

Skull
Move your hands gently over the head to find bleeding, swelling, any soft areas or dents that might indicate a fracture.

Ears
Look for any sign of blood or clear fluids or a mixture of both. Speak, to make sure the casualty can hear in both ears.

Face
Note the colour, temperature and state of the skin. Is it dry or sweaty, flushed or pale, hot or cold?

Look for clues in the casualty's face.

Compare one side with the other.

Eyes
Examine both eyes together, checking the size of the pupil. Look for any wounds or bruising in the whites of the eyes.

Nose
Look for damage and signs of blood, clear fluid or a mixture of both.

Mouth
Note whether the casualty's breathing is easy or difficult, noisy or quiet, fast or slow. Smell the breath. Look for anything in the casualty's mouth that might cause a problem. Examine the casualty's lips for burns and check their colour, looking particularly for blueness. If the casualty is wearing false teeth, leave them in place if possible.

Neck
Loosen any clothing round the casualty's neck. Take off scarves or ties. Look for a medical warning necklace. Look for a stoma (a hole in the windpipe left after surgery). Check the casualty's pulse; is it fast or slow, strong or weak, regular or irregular? Run your fingers down the spine from the base of the skull to between the shoulders, looking for tenderness, unusual bumps or bruising.

Back and spine
Very carefully pass your hand under the hollow of the casualty's back, and feel along their spine, looking for tenderness, unusual bumps, bruising or bleeding.

Look for unusual bumps or bruising.

Chest
Watch the casualty breathing. Does their chest move normally and easily? Does it move on both sides or just one? Check the casualty's collar bones and shoulders for tenderness or bumps. Feel the ribcage for tenderness, bruising or unusual bumps and look for any wounds.

Upper limbs
Check the casualty's upper limbs for movement and feeling.
Can the casualty feel normally, and bend and straighten their fingers and elbows? Note the colour of the casualty's fingers. Check for bruising, swelling, deformity, and for needle marks on the arms. Look for a medical warning bracelet.

Abdomen
Gently feel the soft part of the casualty's abdomen and pelvis, looking for wounds, tenderness, or bruising. Has the casualty been incontinent (that is, have they wet themselves or had their bowels open).

Lower limbs
Ask the casualty to raise each leg in turn, and check they can bend and straighten their ankles and knees. Look for wounds, swelling, or deformity.

Feet
Check for movement and feeling in all the casualty's toes. Check their toe colour, looking particularly for blueness.

Feel carefully for swelling, unusual bumps or bruising.

Personal belongings
Sometimes you may need to search a casualty's pockets or bag to find clues to their condition. If possible, try to do this when someone else is present, preferably an adult. Look after the casualty's possessions, and make sure they are taken with the casualty to hospital or are handed over to the police.

Removing clothing

You may sometimes need to remove the casualty's clothing to examine them properly. Only remove what is absolutely necessary and try to give the casualty privacy wherever possible. Do not tear or damage clothing (although in some cases it may be necessary to cut along the seams of sleeves).

Be sensitive if you are treating someone of the opposite sex, particularly if you need to examine them.

Remember these simple guidelines:
- Always support any injured arms or legs while removing clothing and footwear.
- It is easier to remove an uninjured arm from a sweater, shirt or jacket first and then slip the garment off the injured arm.
- Protective helmets should be left on unless the casualty is having problems breathing. If you do need to remove a helmet, it should be done by two people, one supporting the head and neck while the other undoes the straps and eases the helmet off.
- You may be able to use items of clothing, such as a coat or belt to support fractures if you do not have enough first aid equipment.

Recording information

When you phone 999, it is important to give as much information as possible to ambulance control. It is equally important to tell the ambulance crew (or other qualified medical helpers) as much as you can when you pass the casualty over to their care.

If you have time, try to make a note of the following;
- The casualty's age, name and address.
- What has happened.
- What the condition of the casualty is, details of any injuries and your diagnosis.
- What treatment has been given and when.
- The amount of any medication given to the casualty and the time it was given.
- Any changes that have occurred in the casualty's condition.
- A record of the casualty's breathing, pulse rate and level of response, taken every ten minutes.

Airway and breathing problems

5

We have learnt that everybody needs oxygen to live. Breathing air into the lungs to supply oxygen to the blood then breathing the 'used' air out again is called **respiration**. The 'used' air carries waste products transferred from the blood in the form of carbon dioxide.

The respiratory system is made up of the mouth, nose, windpipe (trachea), lungs and blood vessels. When we breathe in, air passes in through the mouth and nose into the windpipe and down into the lungs. In the lungs are bunches of air sacs called alveoli where the oxygen and carbon dioxide are exchanged. When we breathe out, the air passes up through the windpipe and out of the mouth and nose.

Breathing is controlled by the brain. The lungs themselves do not have any muscles. The breathing action is controlled by the diaphragm (a sheet of muscle which forms the floor of the chest) and by muscles between the ribs.

BREATHING IN (INSPIRATION)

The rib muscles contract, moving the ribs up and out, and the diaphragm contracts and moves down. This makes the space inside the chest bigger, so the pressure is greater outside than inside the lungs. Air flows into the lungs to make the pressure equal.

BREATHING OUT (EXPIRATION)

The rib muscles relax, moving the ribs down and in, and the diaphragm relaxes and moves back up. This makes the space in the chest smaller so the air pressure in the lungs is greater than outside the body. Air flows out to make the pressure equal.

One respiration is breathing in and breathing out. In adults this will take place about 16 times a minute. In children, it is faster at about 20–30 times a minute. The brain changes the rate automatically if levels of oxygen or carbon dioxide in the air are changed or during exercise or injury.

If someone's respiration is disturbed for any reason there is a danger that they may die. This is because the disturbance causes the amount of oxygen in the blood to fall so that not enough oxygen reaches the brain.

There are many reasons for not enough oxygen being carried by the blood:

- Not enough oxygen in the air because of smoke or fumes.
- The casualty's nose, mouth or airway getting blocked.
- Something (such as carbon monoxide gas) affecting the blood in a way that stops it carrying oxygen.
- The casualty's chest wall being crushed or injured.

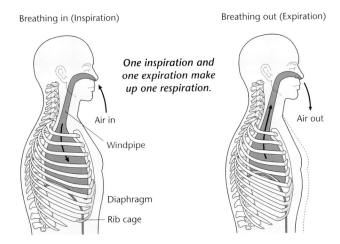

Breathing in (Inspiration)

Breathing out (Expiration)

One inspiration and one expiration make up one respiration.

Air in

Windpipe

Diaphragm

Rib cage

Air out

- The part of the casualty's brain that controls respiration being damaged by a head injury or by poisoning.
- The casualty's lungs not working properly because of an injury or an illness such as pneumonia.

In this chapter we will look at the sort of breathing disorders you may have to deal with as a first aider and what you should do to help.

CHOKING

Choking is when something gets stuck at the back of a casualty's throat and either completely or partly blocks their airway. The most common cause of choking is food but young children often choke after putting things like pebbles or small toys in their mouths.

Recognition
A casualty who is choking may:
- have difficulty in breathing;
- have difficulty in speaking;
- go red and then blue in the face;
- point at or hold their throat;
- be trying to cough something out.

Your aims are to
- remove the obstruction; and
- keep the airway open.

How you can help a choking adult
- Reassure the casualty and encourage them to cough.
- Bend them forwards and give them up to five slaps between their shoulder blades.
- See if you can now remove the obstruction.

If back-slapping does not work, give the casualty up to five abdominal thrusts. To do this:
- Stand behind the casualty.
- Put your arms round their middle. Make a fist with one hand, then grasp your fist with your other hand and place the linked hands just below the ribcage.
- Pull sharply inwards and upwards.

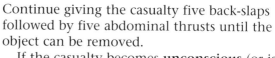

Continue giving the casualty five back-slaps followed by five abdominal thrusts until the object can be removed.

If the casualty becomes **unconscious** (or is unconscious when you find them) you should follow the resuscitation sequence.

If you find that you cannot give the casualty mouth-to-mouth ventilations, you should:
- Turn the casualty onto their side.
- Give them up to five slaps between their shoulder blades.
- See if you can now remove the obstruction.

If the back-slapping does not work, give the casualty up to five abdominal thrusts. To do this when the casualty is lying down:
- Turn the casualty onto their back.
- Kneel astride or alongside the casualty.
- Put the heel of your hand below their ribcage and cover it with your other hand.
- Push your hands down and towards the casualty's head.

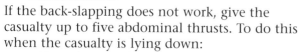

If the casualty is still not breathing, phone 999 for an ambulance. Then give five back-slaps followed by five abdominal thrusts until:

- you find you can give mouth-to-mouth ventilations;
- the casualty begins to breathe normally; or
- help arrives.

How you can help a choking baby
Remember, a baby is an infant under one year old.

- Lay the baby face-down along your forearm. The baby's head should be low.
- Support the baby's back and head.
- Give up to five back-slaps between the baby's shoulder blades.
- Check the baby's mouth and remove any obvious obstruction.

If this does not work, turn the baby over onto their back and give up to five *chest thrusts. Do not give abdominal thrusts to babies*.

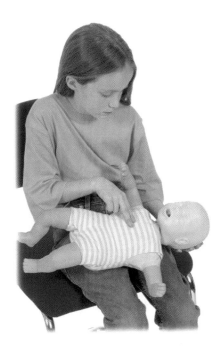

The **chest thrust** is similar to the chest compressions for a baby described in the chapter on CPR. You should push downwards with your fingertips on the baby's chest, one finger's width below the 'nipple line'.

Check the baby's mouth and remove any obvious obstruction.

If the baby is still choking, give five more back-slaps followed by five chest thrusts. Then carry the baby to a telephone and phone 999 for an ambulance.

Continue repeating the sequence of five back-slaps followed by five chest thrusts until help arrives.

If the baby stops breathing, follow the resuscitation sequence.

How you can help a choking child
Remember, a child is someone between one and seven years old.

If the child is conscious:
- Encourage the child to cough if they can.
- Bend the child forwards, with their head lower than their chest and give up to five slaps between the shoulder blades.
- Check the child's mouth and remove any obvious obstruction.

If the back-slapping does not work, give the child up to five chest thrusts. To do this if the child is standing up:
- Stand or kneel behind the child.
- Make a fist of one hand and put it against the child's lower breastbone.
- Grasp your fist with your other hand.
- Press your fist onto the child's chest with a sharp inward thrust.
- Give the chest thrusts at a rate of about one every three seconds.
- Check the child's mouth and remove any obvious obstruction.

If the chest thrusts do not work, give the child another five back-slaps.

Check the child's mouth again and if you still can't clear the obstruction, give up to five abdominal thrusts. To do this:

- Stand or kneel behind the child.
- Make a fist of one hand and put it against the child's lower abdomen.
- Grasp your fist with your other hand.
- Press into the child's abdomen with a sharp upward thrust.

Don't!

try to remove anything from a baby or child's mouth if there is *any* risk that you might push the object down the casualty's throat. *Never* touch the back of a baby or young child's throat.

If this does not work, phone 999 for an ambulance. Continue repeating the sequence of back-slaps, chest thrusts and abdominal thrusts until help arrives. If the child stops breathing, follow the resuscitation sequence.

If the child is unconscious:
- If someone else is with you, ask them to phone 999 for an ambulance.
- Follow the resuscitation sequence.
- If the child's chest won't rise, turn them on to their side and give up to five slaps between the shoulder blades.

Check the child's mouth and remove any obvious obstruction.
- If the child starts to breathe, put them in the recovery position.
- If the child is still not breathing, try to give up to five mouth-to-mouth ventilations.

If the child's chest still won't rise when you try to give mouth-to-mouth ventilation, give the child up to five chest thrusts. To do this:
- Turn the child onto their back on the floor.
- Give up to five sharp chest thrusts on the child's lower breastbone using the heel of **one** hand, pressing the chest to a third of the depth at a rate of about once every three seconds.

Check the child's mouth and remove any obvious obstruction.
- If the child starts to breathe, put them in the recovery position.
- If the child is still not breathing, try to give up to five mouth-to-mouth ventilations.

If the child's chest still won't rise when you try to give mouth-to-mouth ventilation, give the child up to five abdominal thrusts. To do this:
- Turn the child onto their back on the floor.
- Place the heel of your hand midway between child's belly button and breastbone, and give up to five firm abdominal thrusts, using one hand only.

Check the child's mouth and remove any obvious obstruction.
- If the child starts to breathe, put them in the recovery position.
- If the child is still not breathing, try to give up to five mouth-to-mouth ventilations.

If the child's chest still won't rise when you try to give mouth-to-mouth ventilation, phone 999 for an ambulance. Then continue repeating the sequence of back slaps, chest thrusts and abdominal thrusts until help arrives.

When the child is unconscious, follow these four steps to check their condition after each step in the main sequence.
1   Check the child's mouth and remove any obvious obstruction carefully.
2   If the child starts to breathe, put them in the recovery position.
3   If the child is still not breathing, try to give up to five mouth-to-mouth ventilations.
4   If the child's chest won't rise when you try to give mouth-to-mouth ventilation, follow the next step of the main sequence.

DROWNING

A lot of people think that when someone drowns, their lungs become full of water. But usually their throat muscles go into spasm – that means the muscles automatically close the airway – so no water or air can get into their lungs. Without oxygen, of course, the casualty will become unconscious and soon die.

The water that gushes out of a rescued casualty's mouth usually comes from their stomach, not their lungs. That is why you should not waste time trying to get water out of the casualty's lungs. Let the water from the stomach drain out by itself – trying to force it out could push it into the airway and make things worse.

Open the casualty's airway.

Recognition

A casualty who is drowning (or has nearly drowned) may:
- be near, beside or in water;
- be exhausted;
- be coughing and spluttering;
- be unconscious.

If they have been in the water for a long time or if the water is very cold, the casualty may also be suffering from hypothermia (described in chapter **10**).

Don't!
- go in the water unless you are a good swimmer and absolutely *sure it is safe* to do so.
- waste time trying to get water out of the casualty's lungs or stomach.

Your aims are to
- keep the casualty's airway open; and
- get them to hospital.

How you can help at a drowning incident

Rescue the casualty or help them get out of the water if necessary. But remember *never* put your own life at risk.

When the casualty has been rescued, you can help by:
- Laying the casualty down on coats or a blanket.
- Keeping the casualty's head lower than the rest of their body to help stop vomiting and let any water drain away.
- Assessing the casualty, following the DRABC drill.
- Opening the casualty's airway and resuscitating them if necessary.
- Calling the emergency services.
- Wrapping the casualty against the cold and treating for hypothermia if necessary.
- Making sure the casualty goes to hospital, even if they seem to have fully recovered.

STRANGLING

Strangling is when someone's neck is squeezed so that their airway is closed and no air can reach their lungs. Hanging is when someone's body is suspended by a noose round their neck. Hanging has the same effect as strangling.

Strangling and hanging can both happen accidentally. For instance, someone's tie, scarf or other clothing might get caught on something or be wound into moving machinery.

Sometimes, strangling or hanging incidents will need to be investigated by the police. So do not destroy any evidence that the police may need, such as a knotted rope.

Recognition
A casualty who has been strangled may:
- have something wrapped tightly round their neck;
- have marks round their neck showing that something has been wrapped round, even if has now been removed;
- have a blue-ish colour of their face;
- have a 'puffy' face with the veins raised;
- be unconscious.

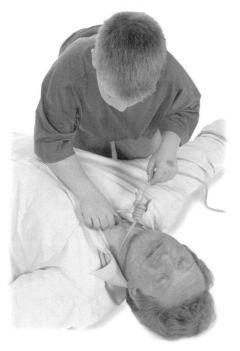

Handy hint!

Sometimes hanging causes other injuries. Try not to move the casualty in case they have a spinal injury.

Your aims are to
- keep the casualty's airway open; and
- get them to hospital.

How you can help a strangled casualty
- Quickly remove anything from round the casualty's neck.
- If the casualty is hanging, support their body.
- Follow the ABC of Resuscitation.
- Phone 999 for an ambulance and make sure the casualty goes to hospital, even if they seem to have fully recovered.

SUFFOCATION

Suffocation is when air can't get to the casualty's lungs because there is something (such as a pillow, plastic bag or sand) covering their nose and mouth.

Recognition
A casualty who is suffocating may:
- have something obviously covering their mouth and nose;
- be struggling to breathe;
- have a blue-ish colour of their face;
- be unconscious.

Your aims are to
- get a supply of air to the casualty's lungs; and
- get them to hospital.

How you can help a suffocating casualty
- Quickly remove anything round the casualty's face, mouth and nose.
- Follow the ABC of Resuscitation.
- Phone 999 for an ambulance and make sure the casualty goes to hospital, even if they seem to have fully recovered.

Someone's airway may also become blocked from other causes. These include:
- Burns in the mouth and throat caused by breathing in smoke and gases or swallowing corrosive chemicals (described in chapter 8).
- Insect stings in the mouth or throat (described in chapter 13).
- Anaphylactic shock (described on the next page).

ANAPHYLACTIC SHOCK

Anaphylactic shock is a very serious allergic reaction. It can affect some people very soon after they are exposed to certain substances if they are sensitive to them. Sometimes, the delay may only be a few seconds.

Among possible causes of anaphylactic shock are:
- getting stung by insects such as wasps;
- eating certain foods such as peanuts;
- injecting drugs.

Handy hint!

People who are sensitive to things like wasp stings often know they are at risk. They may carry adrenaline with them to take in an emergency.

The casualty's airway can become swollen and this can reduce the amount of air getting to their lungs. The casualty will need oxygen urgently and a life-saving injection of a drug called adrenaline.

Recognition
A casualty who is suffering anaphylactic shock may:
- have a swollen face and neck;
- be struggling to breathe;
- have swelling around their eyes;
- be anxious;
- have red, blotchy skin;
- have a fast pulse.

Your aim is
- to get the casualty to hospital *as soon as possible.*

Place an unconscious casualty in the recovery position

How you can help a casualty suffering anaphylactic shock
- Phone 999 for an ambulance (tell the ambulance control officer you think it might be anaphylactic shock).
- If the casualty is conscious, sit them in a position that helps their breathing.
- If the casualty becomes unconscious, follow the ABC of Resuscitation.

SMOKE, FUMES AND GAS

If someone breathes in air containing smoke, gas or solvent fumes, the amount of oxygen getting to their lungs will be reduced.

SMOKE
Recognition
A casualty who has breathed smoke may:
- be struggling to breathe;
- be breathing quickly and noisily;
- cough and wheeze;
- have burns in or around their mouth or nose;
- be unconscious.

Don't! enter a room filled with smoke.

Your aims are to
- help ease the casualty's breathing; and
- get them to hospital.

How you can help a casualty who has breathed smoke
- Phone 999 for an ambulance and the fire service.
- If you are *sure it is safe* to do so, move the casualty from the danger and into fresh air.
- Put out any flames or smouldering on the casualty's clothing.
- If the casualty becomes unconscious, follow the ABC of Resuscitation.
- Treat any burns or other injuries.

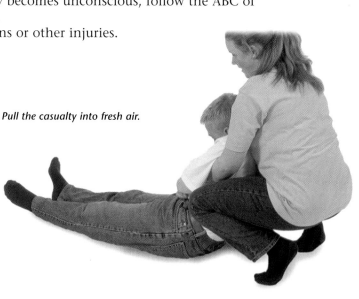

Pull the casualty into fresh air.

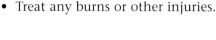

GAS AND FUMES

Recognition

A casualty who has breathed gas or fumes may:
- be struggling to breathe;
- be breathing quickly and noisily;
- have a headache or feel dizzy;
- have a blue-ish colour of their face;
- quickly become unconscious.

Don't! enter a room filled with gas or fumes.

Your aims are to
- help ease the casualty's breathing; and
- get them to hospital.

How you can help a casualty who has breathed gas or fumes
- Phone 999 for an ambulance and the fire service.
- If you are **sure it is safe** to do so, move the casualty from the danger and into fresh air.
- If the casualty becomes unconscious, follow the ABC of resuscitation.

OTHER BREATHING DIFFICULTIES

As a first aider, you may be able to help if someone suddenly has difficulty breathing. People may have difficulty breathing for many reasons, including:
- illnesses such as asthma;
- infections such as bronchitis or croup;
- allergic reactions such as hay fever; and
- hyperventilation.

ASTHMA

When someone suffers an asthma attack, the muscles in their air passages tighten and the lining swells. This makes it very difficult for them to breathe, particularly to breathe out.

Asthma attacks are often triggered by things such as an allergy, cigarette smoke, air pollution or because the sufferer is upset or worried.

People who suffer from asthma usually carry an inhaler with them. The inhaler (which is sometimes called a 'puffer') contains drugs to

Handy hint!

Often asthma sufferers know what is best to ease the attack. So always listen to what the casualty has to say.

help widen the air passages so that the sufferer can breathe more easily. There are two common types of inhaler – the brown inhaler is used at regular intervals to prevent attacks, and the blue inhaler is used during an attack to relieve the symptoms. Large plastic 'spacers' can be fitted to an inhaler to make it easier to use.

Recognition
A casualty who is suffering an asthma attack may:

Let an asthma sufferer sit quietly to recover.

- have a history of asthma;
- be struggling to breathe;
- be breathing noisily or wheezing;
- have a dry, tickly cough;
- find it hard to speak;
- have a blue-ish colour of their face;
- get distressed;
- become unconscious and stop breathing in severe cases.

Your aims are to
- help ease the casualty's breathing; and
- get medical help if needed.

How you can help a casualty who is suffering an asthma attack
- Reassure the casualty and keep them calm.
- Help the casualty to sit down, resting forwards.
- If the casualty has an inhaler, help them to use it.

The casualty's attack should ease after about five to ten minutes. Ask the casualty to take another dose from their inhaler. If the attack goes on for longer or does not ease within five to ten minutes after the casualty has taken their medication, you should:
- Phone 999 for an ambulance.
- Help the casualty to use their inhaler every 5-10 minutes.
- Check the casualty's breathing and pulse every 10 minutes and record your findings.
- Be ready to follow the ABC of Resuscitation if you need to.

HYPERVENTILATION

Hyperventilation means over-breathing. People often hyperventilate if they have had a fright or a panic attack. Hyperventilation can be confused with an asthma attack.

Handy hint!

Hyperventilation can often be confused with asthma. Always check whether the casualty suffers from asthma before you treat them.

Recognition

A casualty who is hyperventilating may:

- be breathing very quickly and deeply;
- be trembling;
- feel dizzy or faint;
- have a tingling feeling or a cramp in their hands and feet.

Your aims are to

- deal with the cause of the casualty's stress; and
- help them calm down.

How you can help a casualty who is hyperventilating

- Reassure the casualty and keep them calm.
- Speak to the casualty firmly but kindly.
- Take the casualty somewhere quiet where they can calm down and control their breathing.
- If the tingling or cramp continues, ask the casualty to breathe out into a paper bag, then breathe the same air back in for a short time. Always make sure you use a paper bag, *not* a plastic bag.

CROUP

Croup is severe breathing difficulty in very young children. It is caused by the child's upper air passages swelling, usually because of infection. Croup attacks usually happen at night. The attack will often ease on its own but if it carries on or if the child has a high temperature, you should call a doctor or ambulance.

Recognition

A child suffering a croup attack may:
- have a cough, like a barking noise;
- make a crowing or whistling noise, especially when they breathe out;
- have a blue-ish colour of their skin;
- be struggling to breathe in severe cases.

Your aims are to
- comfort the child
- get medical help.

Handy hint!

Croup affects very young children so if you have to deal with an attack you probably won't be on your own. Remember to reassure the child's mum and dad, and let them help you care for the child.

How you can help a child who is suffering a croup attack
- Sit the child up, resting back against you.
- Reassure the child and keep them calm.
- Steam will help the child to breathe. Take them into the bathroom or kitchen and run hot water or boil a kettle to produce steam. Let the child breathe in the steamy air. *Be very careful* with hot water and steam.
- Call the doctor.
- If the croup attack is severe, phone 999 for an ambulance.

HICCUPS

Hiccups are short, repeated noisy intakes of air. Almost everyone has had hiccups at some time and most people have their own ways of getting rid of them.

An attack of hiccups doesn't usually last for long. But if it *does* go on for a long time, an attack can be tiring and painful.

Your aim is
- to help ease the hiccups.

Ways to help someone who has hiccups
- Tell them to sit quietly and hold their breath for as long as they can.
- Make them take sips of water from the 'wrong side' of a glass.
- Put a paper bag over their mouth and nose and ask them to breathe in their own air for a short time, as described for hyperventilation. Always make sure you use a paper bag, not a plastic bag.
- If the attack lasts more than a few hours, call a doctor.

Always use a paper bag, never a plastic one.

Circulation problems

6

In this chapter we will look at the sort of circulation disorders first aiders may have to deal with and what they should do to help.

As we saw in the previous chapter, air is breathed into the lungs and oxygen is absorbed by the blood. The blood is then pumped round the body by the heart through a network of blood vessels. This system is known as the circulatory system. There are three types of blood vessels.

Arteries

These are the largest, and take blood containing food and oxygen from the heart to the tissues. Their walls are strong and muscular because blood passing through the arteries is under high pressure and moving fast. Arteries divide down into smaller and smaller vessels, the smallest of which are the capillaries.

Capillaries

These deliver food and oxygen to the body's cells and collect waste products. They eventually join up to become veins.

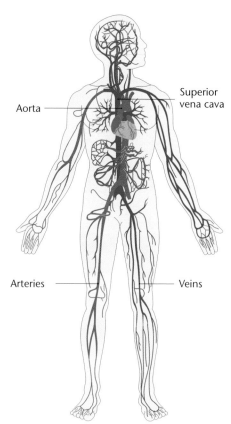

Aorta

Superior vena cava

Veins

These take blood away from the tissues back to the heart. They have thinner, less firm walls as the blood is travelling at a lower pressure. They also contain one-way valves to keep the blood flowing towards the heart.

BLOOD

Blood is made up of red cells, white cells and platelets floating in a liquid called plasma.

Arteries

Veins

Red blood cells are small and round. They contain haemoglobin which carries the oxygen to all parts of the body. This gives the cells their red colour, making the blood look red.

White blood cells are larger and a more irregular shape. They help the body to fight against infection.

Platelets are much smaller, and help to heal any wounds you may have.

Plasma is mostly water. It carries digested food to the cells and collects their waste products.

An average adult will have about six litres (10 pints) of blood which is about one pint of blood for each stone (14lbs) of body weight. A few drops of blood will contain about 5,000 million red blood cells and about 11 million white cells.

THE HEART

The heart is about the size of a clenched fist and weighs about 300 grams (10 ounces) in a healthy adult. It is made from strong heart muscle and constantly pumps blood around the body.

The heart is divided into four chambers: left and right atria (one is called an atrium) and left and right ventricles. With each beat of the heart, blood enters the right atrium from the veins, and flows through a valve into the right ventricle. From here it is pumped through another valve into the pulmonary artery and out to the lungs. In the lungs, the blood picks up more oxygen, and returns to the heart into the left atrium. It then flows through another valve into the left ventricle, where it is pumped through a fourth valve out into the aorta. This is the largest artery in the body and from here it travels out into the body.

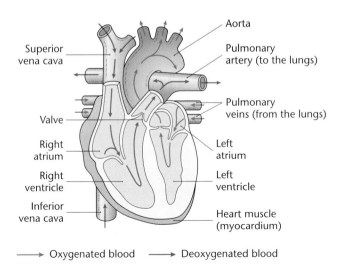

Superior vena cava

Aorta

Pulmonary artery (to the lungs)

Valve

Pulmonary veins (from the lungs)

Right atrium

Left atrium

Right ventricle

Left ventricle

Inferior vena cava

Heart muscle (myocardium)

⟶ Oxygenated blood   ⟶ Deoxygenated blood

THE PULSE

Each time blood is pumped out of the heart is one heartbeat. The series of pumping movements can be felt as a pulse.

The pulse can most easily be felt at places where an artery passes close to the surface of the skin. The usual places to feel an adult's pulse are at the wrist (called the *radial* pulse) and on the side of the neck (called the *carotid* pulse). The usual place to feel a baby's pulse is on the inside of the upper arm (called the *brachial* pulse).

In adults the pulse rate is usually between 60-80 beats each minute. It will be faster in children, or slower in very fit adults, particularly those who take part in a lot of sport. The pulse can also change with exercise, fear, blood loss and some illnesses.

How to take someone's radial pulse

The best place to feel is in the hollow of the casualty's wrist at the bottom of their thumb. Use three fingers and press lightly but do not use your own thumb as it has its own pulse.

When taking someone's pulse you should check and make a note of:
- the rate (beats per minute);
- the strength (strong or weak); and
- the rhythm (regular or irregular).

Do not use your own thumb as it has its own pulse.

SHOCK

Most people probably think of 'shock' as a sudden fear or upset. But to a first aider, it means something much more serious than a fright! The medical definition of shock is a drop in the amount of oxygen reaching the body's vital organs (particularly the brain), usually due to a drop in the amount of blood being pumped round the body. Shock can be caused by:
- severe bleeding;
- burns;
- sickness and diarrhoea; or
- a fall in blood pressure due to a heart problem.

Anaphylactic shock (described in the previous chapter) is caused by a serious allergic reaction. It develops very rapidly in people who are sensitive to certain drugs, foods or insect stings.

Recognition

A casualty who is suffering shock may:

- be faint and dizzy, or lose consciousness;
- have fast, shallow breathing;
- have a fast pulse (as the shock gets worse, the pulse will become weaker and may stop);
- be pale, with grey skin and a blue-ish colour at the earlobes and fingernails;
- feel sweaty, cold and clammy;
- be anxious or even aggressive;
- feel thirsty.

Sometimes, casualties suffering from shock may yawn or gasp for air (this is known as 'air hunger').

Handy hint!

Most casualties who have suddenly become ill, had an accident or been injured will be also suffering from shock. So always follow the treatment for shock as well as dealing with the illness or injury.

Don't!

- use a hot water bottle or electric blanket to warm casualties suffering shock.
- let casualties eat, drink or smoke
- leave the casualties by themselves.

Your aims are to

- improve the supply of oxygen to the vital organs by treating the cause of the shock; and
- get the casualty to hospital as soon as possible.

How you can help a casualty suffering shock

- If you know the cause of the shock, treat it (by controlling bleeding, for example).
- Lay the casualty on a blanket if possible, keeping their head low and their legs supported in a raised position to help blood reach the brain.
- Loosen tight clothing around the casualty's neck, chest and waist.
- Cover the casualty with a blanket or coat.
- Phone 999 for an ambulance.
- Check and record the breathing and pulse every 10 minutes.
- If the casualty becomes unconscious, follow the ABC of Resuscitation.

FAINTING

Fainting is a short period of unconsciousness caused by a drop in the supply of blood to the brain. Fainting may be caused by pain, fright, lack of food or emotional upset. The casualty usually quickly recovers.

Recognition
A casualty who has fainted may:
- briefly lose consciousness;
- have a slow pulse;
- have pale sweaty skin.

To decide whether a casualty has fainted or is suffering from shock, remember the *pulse* is usually *fast in shock, slow with fainting*.

Your aims are to
- reassure the casualty; and
- improve the supply of oxygen to the brain.

How you can help a fainting casualty
- Lay the casualty down and raise and support their legs.
- Make sure the casualty has plenty of fresh air.
- As the casualty recovers, reassure them and help them to sit up slowly.
- Check for any injuries caused by falling and treat if needed.
- If the casualty does not start to recover after a short time or remains unconscious, follow the ABC of Resuscitation.
- Phone 999 for an ambulance if needed.

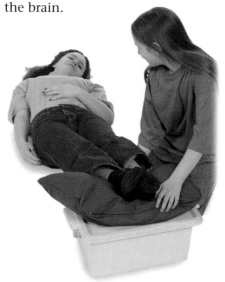

If someone has fainted, keep their legs raised slightly.

If the casualty, having partly recovered, feels faint again, lay them down and raise and support their legs, until they are fully recovered.

HEART DISORDERS

ANGINA PECTORIS

Angina pectoris is a pain in the chest caused by a drop in the amount of oxygen reaching an area of heart muscle, usually because one or more of the arteries supplying the blood is narrowed. The attack usually makes the casualty stop to rest. Some casualties carry medication to help the pain.

Recognition

A casualty who has angina may:
- have a tight pain in their chest which may spread to their left arm and neck:
- be short of breath;
- feel weak and dizzy.

Your aim is
- to encourage the casualty to rest.

How you can help a casualty with angina
- Help the casualty to sit down and reassure them.
- Help the casualty take their medication (tablets, a spray or a 'puffer') if they have any.
- Let the casualty rest.
- If the angina attack doesn't settle within a few minutes or if the pain carries on or gets worse, phone 999 for an ambulance.
- Check and record the casualty's breathing and pulse.
- If the casualty becomes unconscious, follow the ABC of Resuscitation.

Angina is painful but rest should help.

HEART ATTACKS

A heart attack is caused when one or more of the arteries supplying blood to the heart muscle becomes blocked. How serious the heart attack is will depend on how much heart muscle is affected – it may involve the whole heart or just a small area of it.

The medical term for a heart attack is *myocardial infarction* and it shows itself as severe pain in the chest – but unlike angina, rest will not ease the pain.

Recognition

A casualty who is having a heart attack may suddenly collapse. They will have a severe pain in their chest which may spread to their left arm and neck and also may:

- be short of breath;
- feel weak and dizzy.
- be very pale with blue-ish lips;
- have a fast pulse, becoming weaker.

Your aims are to

- encourage the casualty to rest; and
- to get them to hospital *as soon as possible.*

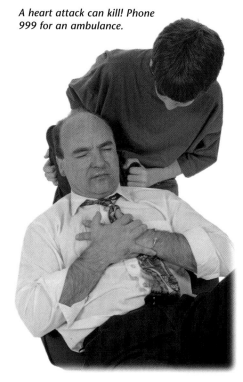

A heart attack can kill! Phone 999 for an ambulance.

How you can help a casualty having a heart attack

- Make the casualty comfortable (half-sitting, with knees bent and head and shoulders supported is often the most comfortable position).
- Reassure the casualty.
- Phone 999 for an ambulance; it is very important to tell the controller you think it is a heart attack so the ambulance crew bring special equipment.
- Check and record the casualty's breathing and pulse every 10 minutes.

- Aspirin may help if the casualty can take it; one tablet should be chewed slowly (remember to tell the ambulance crew if the casualty has taken aspirin).
- If the casualty collapses and becomes unconscious, follow the ABC of Resuscitation.

CARDIAC ARREST
Cardiac arrest is a medical term used when the heart suddenly stops. This may be because of a heart attack, severe bleeding, electric shock, anaphylactic shock or drugs.

Handy hint!

If chest pain is due to angina, it will usually get better after rest and medication. With a heart attack, the pain usually continues and may get worse.

If a casualty suffers a cardiac arrest, resuscitation must be started straight away, as described in chapter 3.

Recognition
A casualty who has suffered a cardiac arrest will:
- not be breathing; and
- have no pulse.

Your aims are to
- start resuscitation as soon as possible; and
- to phone 999 for an ambulance.

How you can help if a casualty suffers a cardiac arrest
- Always check an unconscious casualty's breathing and pulse.
- If breathing is missing, phone 999 for an ambulance and follow the ABC of Resuscitation.

Once an ambulance is on its way, you should continue with resuscitation to keep the casualty's brain supplied with oxygen until help arrives.

DEFIBRILLATORS

A defibrillator is a medical device to give a casualty's heart a controlled electric shock.

When a casualty has had a cardiac arrest, a defibrillator is usually the only way to start their heart beating again. Most ambulances carry a defibrillator. It is very important to tell ambulance control as much as you can about the casualty so that the controller can make sure the right equipment is sent.

A defibrillator should only be used by someone who has been trained.

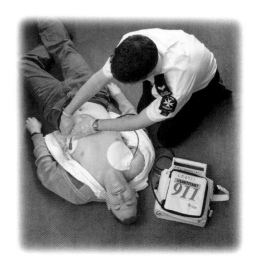

Wounds and bleeding

7

When a blood vessel is damaged blood leaks out, either into the tissues or onto the surface of your skin. The body has a natural reaction to this – platelets collect around the damage and a substance called fibrin is produced by the body.

Fibrin traps blood cells and platelets and forms a clot to protect against infection and to stop the bleeding. The clot dries to make a scab under which new skin or tissue grows. When the scab falls off, the damage is almost healed.

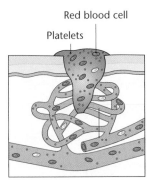

Platelets collect around the injury and produce fibrin.

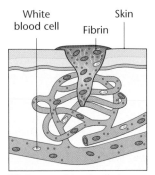

Fibrin traps blood cells to make a clot.

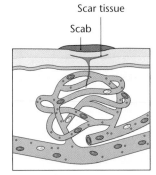

The clot dries to make a scab and new tissue grows underneath.

Sometimes the bleeding may be too heavy to stop on its own and help is needed. Some medical conditions, such as haemophilia or leukaemia, also stop the clotting action from working properly.

TYPES OF BLEEDING

Bleeding differs depending on what type of blood vessel is damaged.

Arterial bleeding is bright red and spurts from the wound in time with the pulse.

Venous bleeding is dark red, because it carries less oxygen. There may be severe blood loss, but at a steadier rate.

Capillary bleeding is more like oozing, and blood loss is slight.

TYPES OF WOUND

There are five main types of wound.

Bruise – capillaries under the skin may ooze blood after a blow, although the skin's surface may not be broken.

Graze – the top layers of skin are scraped off, usually by a sliding fall. The skin looks raw and tender, and often has grit or dirt stuck to it.

Incised – a clean cut, usually caused by a knife, glass or other sharp object. It may be deep, causing damage to muscles and tendons.

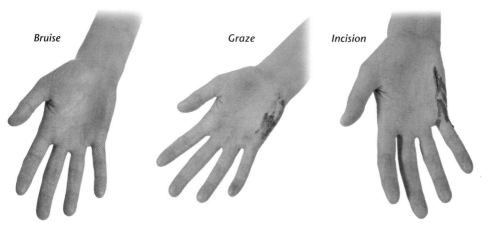

Bruise   *Graze*   *Incision*

Laceration – a ragged tear, usually caused by a rough object, such as barbed wire.

Puncture – usually small but deep, so may cause internal damage. May result from stabbing or standing on a nail.

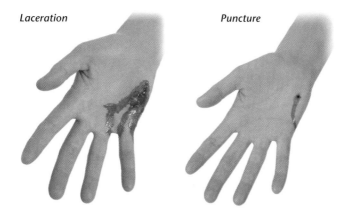

Laceration   *Puncture*

SEVERE EXTERNAL BLEEDING

Severe external bleeding is when blood is pouring from a wound at a fast rate. If an artery has been cut, the blood may spurt out of the wound, like water coming out of a hosepipe.

Recognition
A casualty who has a severe external wound may:
- be losing a lot of blood from the wound (in 'spurts' if an artery is cut);
- have a fast pulse, becoming weaker;
- be pale with blue-ish lips;
- feel sweaty, cold and clammy.

Your aims are to
- control the bleeding;
- prevent shock; and
- get the casualty to hospital.

Handy hint!

If your casualty has a gunshot wound, always check for another wound where the bullet has left the body. Often the entry wound is small, but the exit wound may be large and ragged.

How you can help someone who has a severe external wound
- Check the wound for any object in it, such as glass.
- Put direct pressure on the wound with your fingers or hand (preferably over a clean pad).
- If you cannot use direct pressure because there is something in the wound, press down firmly either side of the object.
- If the wound is on a limb, raise and support it to help slow the blood flow (but be careful in case a bone is broken).
- Help the casualty to lie down, support their legs in a raised position.
- Put a sterile dressing over the wound and bandage it firmly (but not so tightly that it stops the circulation, especially to fingers and toes).
- Phone 999 for an ambulance.
- Treat the casualty for shock.
- Check and record the casualty's breathing and pulse every 10 minutes.

You should also check dressings frequently. If blood is oozing through a dressing, don't remove it from the wound but bandage another dressing on top of the first one. Check that bandages aren't so tight that they interfere with the casualty's circulation; check for a pulse beyond any bandages regularly.

Raise the limb and apply pressure, preferably using a clean pad.

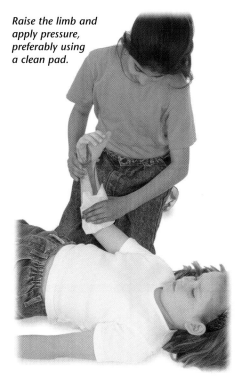
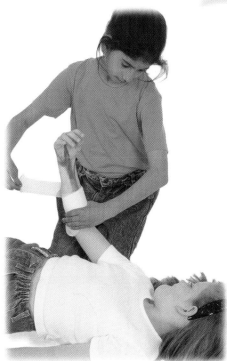

ABDOMINAL WOUNDS

Wounds to the abdomen (the part of the body between the bottom of the ribs and the pelvis) may cause bleeding and damage to organs such as the spleen, liver, kidneys or intestines. Abdominal wounds may be caused by crushing injuries, stabbing or even by gunshots.

Recognition
The casualty's history may reveal an abdominal wound, and the casualty also may:
- be bleeding from the abdominal area;
- have organs, such as the intestines, showing through the wound;
- be suffering from shock.

Your aims are to
- stop or control the bleeding;
- keep the wound as clean as possible;
- prevent shock; and
- get the casualty to hospital.

How you can help someone who has an abdominal wound

- Lay the casualty down on a blanket if possible.
- Put a large dressing on the wound, and keep it in place with a bandage or strapping.
- If organs, such as the intestines, are showing through the wound do not touch them but cover them with kitchen film or a plastic bag before putting a dressing on.

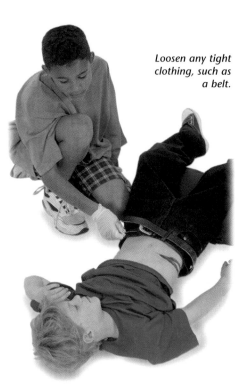

Loosen any tight clothing, such as a belt.

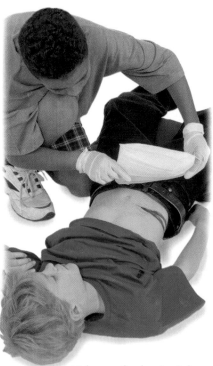

Make sure the dressing is large enough to cover the wound.

- If the casualty coughs or is sick, press firmly on the dressing to stop the intestines coming through the wound.
- If the wound cuts across the abdomen, bend and support the casualty's knees to ease the strain on the injury. *Do not* raise the knees if the wound is *vertical*.
- Phone 999 for an ambulance.
- Treat the casualty for shock.
- Check and record the casualty's breathing and pulse every 10 minutes.

CHEST WOUNDS

Wounds to the chest may cause bleeding and damage to the lungs. This can cause problems with breathing. If the wound is deep enough, air will enter and may cause the lung to collapse.

Recognition

The casualty's history may reveal a chest wound, and the casualty also may:

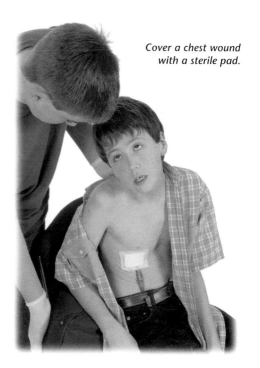

Cover a chest wound with a sterile pad.

- be bleeding from the chest area;
- have difficulty breathing;
- find it painful to breathe;
- be coughing up bright red frothy blood;
- be pale or a blue-ish colour;
- make sounds as air is sucked into the wound when they breathe in;
- be suffering from shock.

Your aims are to

- control the bleeding;
- help the casualty breathe more comfortably;
- prevent shock; and
- get the casualty to hospital.

How you can help someone with a chest wound

- Cover the wound immediately, using either the palm of the casualty's hand or the palm of your own.
- Put a sterile dressing or pad over the wound, cover this with a plastic bag, kitchen film or foil, and secure it with strapping on three sides to stop air being drawn into the wound.
- Help the casualty to find the most comfortable position (often half-sitting and leaning towards the injured side).
- Phone 999 for an ambulance.
- Treat the casualty for shock.
- If the casualty becomes unconscious, follow the ABC of Resuscitation.

CRUSH INJURIES

Crush injuries are usually caused by things like car or train crashes, accidents on building sites, buildings collapsing, or explosions.

It is important not to try and free a casualty who has been crushed for more than 10 minutes unless skilled medical help is on hand. This is because serious problems may have developed and these will need treatment by a doctor or other specialist.

Recognition
The casualty's history may reveal a crush injury. The casualty also may:
- be bleeding severely;
- have broken bones;
- be suffering from shock.

Your aim is to
- get specialist medical help immediately.

How you can help someone who has been crushed for *LESS* than 10 minutes
- Free the casualty if you can.
- Treat any bleeding and cover any wounds.
- Treat any fractures.
- Phone 999 for an ambulance.
- Check and record the casualty's breathing and pulse every 10 minutes.
- Record how long the casualty was trapped for and the time they were freed.

How you can help someone who has been crushed for *MORE* than 10 minutes
- *Do not* try to free the casualty.
- Phone 999 for an ambulance, giving as much information as you can.
- Treat any injuries and shock as far as you can.
- Reassure the casualty.

ACCIDENTAL AMPUTATION

Amputation is when a limb, or part of a limb (such as a finger) is cut or torn off in an accident. Sometimes, the injured part is cut off completely (*complete amputation*) and sometimes it is still attached by tissue or skin (*partial amputation*).

Don't! wash the severed part, put cotton wool on any wound, or let the crushed ice touch the severed part.

It may be possible for the severed part to be re-attached using micro-surgery. The sooner the casualty gets to hospital, the more chance there is of surgery succeeding.

Recognition
As well as obvious signs, such as a missing finger or severe bleeding, the casualty also may:
- be very pale;
- have sweaty, cold, clammy skin;
- be suffering from shock.

Your aims are
- to control bleeding;
- to treat shock;
- to find and carefully look after the severed part; and
- to phone 999 for an ambulance.

How you can help someone who has suffered an accidental amputation
- Treat the bleeding by applying direct pressure and by raising the injured limb.
- Put a sterile dressing or clean pad on the wound.
- Treat the casualty for shock.
- Phone 999 for an ambulance (remember to tell the controller about the amputation).
- Wrap the severed part in kitchen film or put it in a clean plastic bag.
- Wrap it again in soft material, such as a clean teatowel, and put in another clean plastic bag, filled with crushed ice.
- Put a label on the package, stating the casualty's name and the time when the injury happened.
- Make sure you give the package to the ambulance crew.

INTERNAL BLEEDING

By internal bleeding, we mean bleeding inside the body. It can be very serious.

Because you cannot see internal bleeding, it can be easily missed when you are treating a casualty.

Internal bleeding can be caused by fractures of bones such as the ribs and the thighbone, or by illness such as a stomach ulcer, or by certain drugs.

Recognition
The casualty's history may reveal an injury, illness or drug-taking and the casualty also may:

- have a fast, weak pulse;
- be pale, with cold clammy skin;
- be bleeding from the mouth or have blood in their urine;
- feel pain, particularly in the chest or abdomen;
- be confused and restless;
- become unconscious.

Handy hint!

The casualty's history is important. There may be marks on their chest or abdomen to make you suspect internal injury. If a casualty is getting worse and you can't find anything obviously wrong, you should always suspect internal bleeding.

Your aims are to
- treat the shock; and
- get the casualty to hospital.

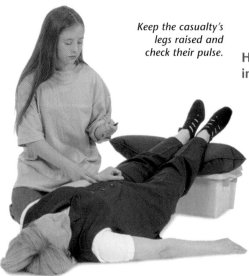

Keep the casualty's legs raised and check their pulse.

How you can help someone with internal bleeding
- Help the casualty to lie down (on a blanket if possible) and raise and support their legs.
- Phone 999 for an ambulance.
- Treat the casualty for shock.
- Check and record the casualty's breathing, pulse and level of response every 10 minutes.
- If the casualty becomes unconscious, follow the ABC of Resuscitation.

BLEEDING FROM THE MOUTH

Bleeding from the mouth is usually caused by the casualty biting their lip, tongue or cheek, perhaps after a fall or fight. If a tooth is knocked out accidentally (or taken out by a dentist) there may be bleeding from the tooth socket.

Use a gauze swab to soak up the blood.

Recognition
The casualty's history may reveal a fall or other injury, and the casualty also may:
- be bleeding from the mouth;
- have problems with breathing if the bleeding is severe.

Your aims are to
- stop the bleeding; and
- keep the casualty's airway open.

How you can help someone whose mouth is bleeding
- Help the casualty to sit down, with their head leaning forward and towards the injured side to let the blood drain out of their mouth.
- Put a gauze pad over the wound and ask the casualty to squeeze it between finger and thumb to stop the bleeding.
- If the bleeding is from a tooth socket, put a gauze pad over the socket and ask the casualty to bite on the pad.
- If the bleeding continues, replace the pad.
- Ask the casualty not to swallow but let any blood trickle out of their mouth into a tissue or bowl.
- If the wound is large or the bleeding continues, get the casualty to hospital or to a dentist.
- Severe bleeding may cause problems with breathing so be prepared to follow the ABC of Resuscitation.

How you can help someone who has had a tooth knocked out
If an adult's tooth gets knocked out, it should be re-planted into its socket as soon as possible (but a child's milk tooth should *not* be re-planted).
- *Do not* try to clean the tooth.
- Put the tooth back in the socket, keeping it pressed in place with a gauze swab.
- Get the casualty to a dentist or hospital as soon as possible.
- If the tooth will not stay in place, put it in a container of milk and take it to the dentist or hospital with the casualty.

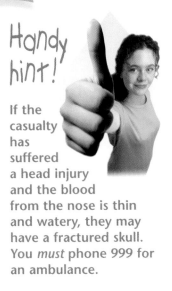

Handy hint!

If the casualty has suffered a head injury and the blood from the nose is thin and watery, they may have a fractured skull. You *must* phone 999 for an ambulance.

NOSEBLEEDS

There are several possible causes of a nosebleed. The casualty may have fallen over and banged their nose or may have been hit on the nose. Picking your nose can make it bleed and so can blowing it too often when you have a cold.

Recognition
The casualty's history may reveal an injury and there will be bleeding from the casualty's nose.

Your aims are to
- stop the bleeding; and
- keep the casualty's airway open.

How you can help someone with a nosebleed
- Help the casualty sit down and loosen any tight clothing around their neck.
- Lean the casualty forward and pinch their nostrils together just below the bony bit of their nose.
- Keep the pressure on for at least 10 minutes, asking the casualty to breathe through their mouth.
- Ask the casualty not to sniff, swallow, cough or blow their nose because it may disturb blood clots.
- Release the pressure after 10 minutes but if the casualty's nose is still bleeding, keep the pressure on for a further 10 minutes.
- If the nosebleed does not stop after 30 minutes, get medical advice.

Pinch the nostrils to help stop a nosebleed.

EMBEDDED OBJECTS

An embedded object is something that is stuck in a wound. It could be a piece of broken glass or a sharp bit of metal. You should **not** try to pull the object out because this may cause more damage and make the bleeding worse.

Recognition

The casualty's history may suggest an embedded object or you may see it sticking out of the wound.

Your aims are to

- stop the bleeding without disturbing the object in the wound; and
- keep the wound clean.

Apply pressure either side of an embedded object.

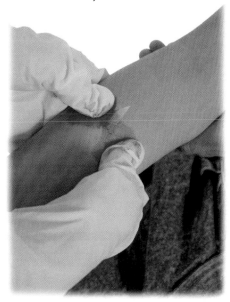

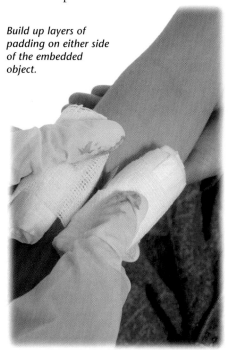

Build up layers of padding on either side of the embedded object.

How you can help someone with an object embedded in a wound

- **Do not** try to remove the object.
- Press down on either side of the object.
- Raise and support the injured part to help control the bleeding, taking care in case there is a fracture.
- Gently cover the wound and the object with a clean dressing then, taking care not to disturb the dressing or object, build up layers of padding on either side of the object and bandage.
- Get the casualty to hospital.

SPLINTERS

A splinter is a small piece of wood, metal or glass stuck in a wound, usually just underneath the skin. Sometimes part of the splinter is sticking out so it can be easily pulled out using tweezers.

Handy hint!

If there is grit and mud in a small wound, it can be cleaned by soaking in warm soapy water. Often the grit and mud will float out of the wound.

Recognition
The casualty's history may suggest a splinter or you may see it sticking out.

Your aims are to
- remove the splinter if you can; and
- keep the wound clean.

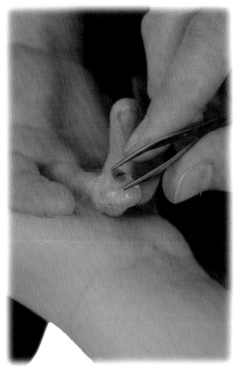

Remove a splinter by pulling gently at the same angle it went in.

How you can help someone with a splinter
- Clean the area around the splinter with soap and warm water.
- Get hold of the splinter with clean tweezers and gently pull it out at the same angle that it went in.
- Squeeze the wound to make it bleed a little.
- Clean and dry the wound and put a plaster over it.
- Check whether the casualty has been inoculated against tetanus – if not, or if the inoculation is not up-to-date, advise the casualty to see their doctor.
- If the splinter does not come out easily, or if it breaks up, treat it as an embedded object.

MINOR BLEEDING

It is usually easy to stop minor bleeding by applying pressure and by raising the injured part. Usually minor wounds will only need a plaster and won't need to be seen by a doctor.

Recognition
There will be signs of slight bleeding which may have already stopped.

Your aims are to
* stop any bleeding; and
* keep the wound clean.

How you can help someone with a minor wound
* Stop any bleeding.
* If the wound is dirty, rinse it under running water.
* Pat it dry with a clean piece of material or a gauze swab.
* Cover the wound with a plaster.

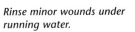

Handy hint!

Remember, protect yourself. Use disposable gloves and cover your cuts with a waterproof plaster.

Rinse minor wounds under running water.

Burns and Scalds

8

Burns destroy the skin. Depending on how deep the burn is, it may cause loss of tissue fluid (serum) and damage nerves and blood vessels. There is also risk of infection because the natural barrier has been broken. If the airway has been burned, the casualty may have difficulty breathing.

THE SKIN

Our skin is the waterproof, flexible covering that protects the body from the outside world and helps keep out harmful bacteria.

It also lets us sense what is happening around us because it is sensitive to touch, cold, heat, pressure and pain.

Human skin is formed of several layers. The outer layer is called the **epidermis** and its surface is the part we see and feel. It contains a special fatty substance that makes the skin waterproof. Cells in the lower part of the epidermis are continually multiplying, and gradually moving outwards, where they flake away on reaching the surface.

The inner layer is called the **dermis**. This contains blood vessels, nerves, muscles, sweat glands, and hair follicles.

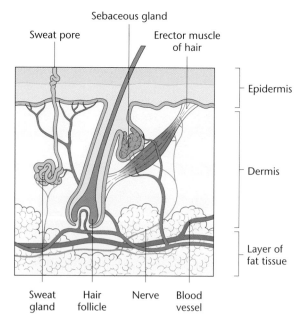

Sebaceous gland

Sweat pore

Erector muscle of hair

Epidermis

Dermis

Layer of fat tissue

Sweat gland   Hair follicle   Nerve   Blood vessel

Below the dermis is a layer of **adipose tissue** or fat, which provides insulation and stores food. It is thicker on some parts of the body than others, and women tend to have more than men.

TYPES OF BURN

Burns are caused by dry heat, such as flames, friction or extreme cold. Scalds are caused by wet heat, such as hot liquids or steam. The principles of treatment are the same for both.

There are three types of burn or scald, depending on their depth.

Superficial – involves the outer surface of skin only. A superficial burn looks red and swollen and is painful. It needs medical help only if it covers a large area.

Partial-thickness – involves the epidermis layer. It looks raw, may cause blisters, and needs medical help.

Full-thickness – involves all layers of skin and may damage nerves or muscles. It looks pale or blackened like charring and needs urgent medical help

Superficial burn

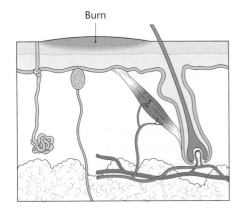

Burn

Partial-thickness burn

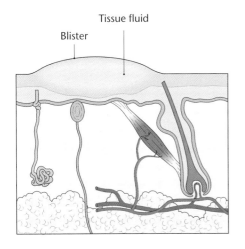

Tissue fluid

Blister

Full-thickness burn

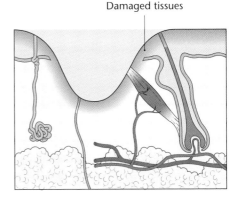

Damaged tissues

THE RULE OF NINES

The body can be divided into areas of about 9 per cent of skin area. For instance, the head is 9 per cent and so is one arm. The back is 18 per cent – in other words, two times 9 per cent. A hand is equal to about one per cent. This 'rule of nines' helps first aiders to decide what medical help is needed.

- A partial-thickness burn covering more than **one per cent** of an adult's skin should be seen by a **doctor**.
- A partial-thickness burn covering more than **nine per cent** of an adult's skin needs **hospital** treatment.
- Any **full-thickness** burn needs **hospital** treatment.
- Any partial- or full-thickness burns to a **child** need **hospital** treatment.

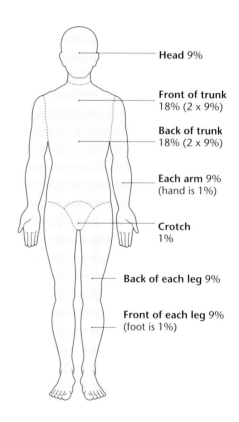

Head 9%

Front of trunk 18% (2 x 9%)

Back of trunk 18% (2 x 9%)

Each arm 9% (hand is 1%)

Crotch 1%

Back of each leg 9%

Front of each leg 9% (foot is 1%)

SEVERE BURNS AND SCALDS

A severe burn or scald is a partial-thickness or full-thickness burn or a superficial burn involving a large area. The casualty may also be suffering from shock.

Don't!
- touch the injured area;
- burst any blisters;
- use lotions, ointments, creams or sticky tape;
- remove anything sticking to the burn.

Recognition
Refer to the section on the previous page on types of burns.

Your aims are to
- stop the burning and ease the pain;
- treat shock; and
- get the casualty to hospital.

How you can help someone who has severe burns
- Put your DRABC drill into practice.
- Start cooling the burn at once by flooding the area with plenty of cold liquid.
- Make the casualty comfortable, laying them down if possible but protecting the burn from the ground.
- Phone 999 for an ambulance.
- Continue to cool the burn with cold liquid – this will take at least ten minutes but try not to let the casualty get too cold.
- Remove the casualty's jewellery, watch and clothing from the affected area unless they are sticking to the skin.
- Cover the burn with clean, non-fluffy material to protect from infection (a clean teatowel, a plastic bag or cling film all make good dressings for burns).
- Treat the casualty for shock.
- Check and record the casualty's breathing and pulse every 10 minutes.
- If the casualty becomes unconscious, follow the ABC of Resuscitation.

Cool the burned area with lots of cold water.

Handy hint!

Remember burns to the face and mouth may cause swelling and block the airway. Follow the DRABC drill and get medical help urgently if needed.

MINOR BURNS AND SCALDS

Minor burns and scalds are superficial burns covering an area smaller than a postage stamp. They do not usually need medical help.

Don't!

•use plasters;
•burst any
  blisters;
•use lotions,
  ointments, creams
  or sticky tape;
•remove anything
  sticking to the
  burn.

Recognition

A casualty with minor burns may:
- have red skin around the injured area;
- have swelling;
- the injured area may feel tender.

Your aims are to
- stop the burning;
- relieve the pain; and
- help prevent infection.

How you can help someone with minor burns or scalds
- Hold the affected area under cold, running water or any other cold harmless liquid (such as milk) for at least 10 minutes or until the pain eases.
- Remove the casualty's jewellery, watch and clothing from the affected area unless it is sticking to the skin.
- Cover the burn with clean, non-fluffy material to protect from infection (a clean teatowel, a plastic bag or cling film all make good dressings for burns).
- Reassure the casualty.

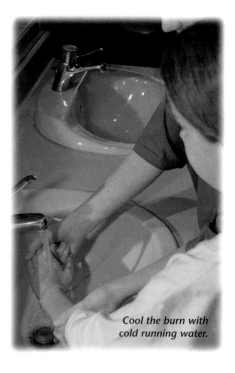

Cool the burn with cold running water.

A clean teatowel, a plastic bag or cling film all make good dressings for burns.

BURNS AFFECTING THE AIRWAY

If someone's face gets burned or if they have breathed in hot air or gas, their mouth and throat may become swollen. This is very dangerous because it makes it difficult for the casualty to breathe. If the swelling is severe, it can completely block the airway and the casualty may suffocate. Urgent medical aid is always needed.

Recognition
A casualty who has burns affecting the airway may have:
- damaged skin or soot around their mouth or nose;
- a red or swollen tongue;
- difficulty with breathing.

Handy hint!

Remember, the treatment for a burn or a scald is the same.

Your aims are to
- keep the airway open; and
- get urgent medical aid.

How you can help someone whose airway is affected by burns
- Phone 999 for an ambulance and tell ambulance control that you suspect burns to the airway.
- Try to improve the air supply to the casualty by loosening tight clothing and moving them into fresh air.
- If the casualty becomes unconscious, follow the ABC of Resuscitation.

ELECTRICAL BURNS

When someone comes into contact with electric current, they may suffer burns. These burns are usually at the places where the current has gone into and out of the casualty's body. But electricity may cause internal damage as well.

Handy hint!

Make sure the liquid used to cool the burns does not come into contact with any electrical appliances.

Recognition
A casualty who has been in contact with electricity may:
- be unconscious;
- have full-thickness burns with swelling and charring at the contact points;
- be suffering from shock.

Your aims are to
- treat the burns;
- treat shock; and
- get the casualty to hospital.

Make sure the power is turned off before you approach the casualty.

Never approach a casualty who has been in contact with high-voltage electricity (such as power lines or railways) until you have been told by an official that the power has been switched off. Stay at least 20 metres away until it is safe.

How you can help a casualty who has been in contact with electricity
- Follow the DRABC drill.
- Use plenty of cold liquid to cool the burns.
- Cover the burn with clean, non-fluffy material to protect it from infection (a clean teatowel, a plastic bag or cling film all make good dressings for burns).
- Phone 999 for an ambulance.
- Treat the casualty for shock.

CHEMICAL BURNS

Many chemicals can cause burns. Some are found in the home, including bleach, oven cleaner, paint stripper and weedkillers. Others are industrial chemicals found in factories or carried in road tankers. The signs of a chemical burn take longer to appear than those from a heat burn. Chemical burns need hospital treatment and it will help if you can tell the hospital the name of the chemical.

Recognition

The casualty's history may reveal contact with chemicals, and the casualty also may:
- have severe, stinging pain;
- develop redness, blistering, peeling and swelling on their skin (although these signs may not appear at once).

Your aims are to
- identify and remove the chemical;
- cool any burns; and
- get the casualty to hospital.

How you can help someone who has been burned by chemicals
- Make sure the area is safe. If you need to move the casualty away from the area, don't forget to protect yourself.
- Cool the casualty's burn by flooding the affected area with cold water. This may take 20 minutes or more because cooling chemical burns is slower than cooling heat burns.

Cool chemical burns with lots of running water.

Handy hint!

Always remember to protect yourself from chemicals. When cooling a burn, try to make sure the water runs *away* **from undamaged skin.**

- Phone 999 for an ambulance.
- Carefully remove any clothing splashed with the chemical. Wear protective gloves to do this.
- Treat the casualty for shock.
- Check and record the casualty's breathing and pulse every 10 minutes.
- If the casualty becomes unconscious, follow the ABC of Resuscitation.

BURNS AFFECTING THE EYES

Burns to the eyes are usually caused by chemical splashes or fireworks. They can cause serious damage if not treated quickly.

Recognition
The casualty's history may reveal the cause of injury (such as contact with chemicals) and their eyes may be watering. The casualty also may:
- feel pain in their eyes or be unable to open them;
- have redness and swelling round the eyes.

Your aims are to
- rinse away any chemicals; and
- get the casualty to hospital.

How you can help someone whose eyes are affected by burns
- Hold the affected eye under gently running cold water for at least 10 minutes.

Keep your hands clear of the rinsing water.

- If the eye is shut, try to gently pull the eyelids open. Keep your hands away from the water.
- Ask the casualty to hold a sterile eye pad or clean non-fluffy material over the affected eye, then bandage it lightly in place if possible.
- Get the casualty to hospital.

Handy hint!

Always remember to protect yourself from chemicals. When cooling, try to make the water drain off the casualty's face without getting in the unaffected eye. It may be easier to pour the water from a glass or jug.

CS GAS

CS 'gas' is a solvent spray, not a true gas. It is used by police officers or soldiers to control suspects or rioters. Sometimes innocent bystanders may be affected by the spray.

If CS gas is sprayed in someone's face, it irritates their eyes and upper airway and leaves them helpless for a short while. The effects usually wear off after about 10 or 15 minutes.

Handy hint!

If someone is an asthma sufferer, contact with CS gas can trigger an attack. Treat the asthma attack in the usual way.

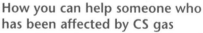

How you can help someone who has been affected by CS gas

- Turn the casualty so that they face into the wind or towards fresh air.
- Ask the casualty not to rub their eyes and face.
- If the irritation doesn't ease, rinse the casualty's eyes and face with plenty of cold water.
- If rinsing the eyes and face does not help, seek medical advice.

SUNBURN

If people stay out in the sun too long without protecting their skin, they may suffer sunburn. It can also be caused by sunlamps.

Recognition
The casualty's history may reveal that they have been out in the sun and the casualty also may have:
- very red skin;
- surface burns on their skin causing itching and tenderness; and
- blisters.

Your aims are to
- move the casualty to a cool place; and
- help cool the burn and relieve pain.

How you can help someone who is suffering from sunburn
- Help the casualty into the shade or indoors.
- Cool their skin by sponging with cold water or soaking in a cool bath for 10 minutes.
- Give the casualty plenty of cold water to drink.
- If the burns are mild, it may help to apply calamine lotion or an after-sun lotion.
- When the skin is blistered, ask the casualty to see a doctor.

Handy hint!

Never stay out in strong sunshine. Protect yourself – use sun protection creams and wear a sunhat

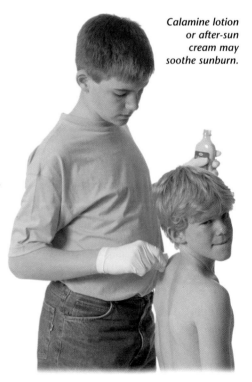

Calamine lotion or after-sun cream may soothe sunburn.

Unconsciousness

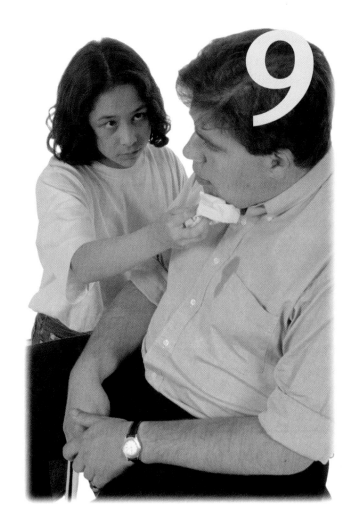

9

The brain is the body's control centre and needs a constant supply of oxygen in the blood to work properly.

Different parts of the brain control the functions of the body, as well as thoughts, feelings and memory.

The nervous system carries messages from the brain to control the body. It makes sure all the different parts work together properly and is divided into systems.

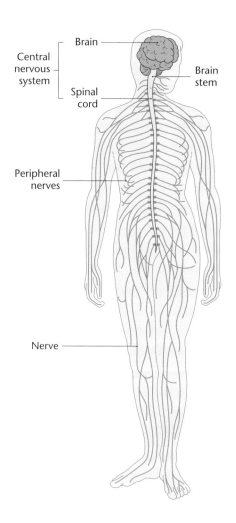

Central nervous system – is made up of the brain and the spinal cord which carries messages between the brain and the body.

Peripheral nervous system – is made up of the nerves coming out of the brain and spinal cord. There are two types of nerves:

- *sensory nerves* carry messages from your skin and sense organs to the central nervous system.
- *motor nerves* carry messages from the central nervous system to the muscles.

Autonomic nervous system – connects the major systems of your body (such as the blood, digestive, and respiratory systems) to the brain and controls automatic activities such as digestion and respiration.

THE SPINAL CORD

This is the thick cord of nerves, running from the brain to the bottom of the back. It is protected by the bones of the spine. Messages between the brain and the peripheral nerves pass through the spinal cord. Injury to the brain and spinal cord is serious because these type of cells rarely recover.

THE BRAIN

The brain is the body's control centre. Different parts of the brain control different parts of the body. As well as keeping your body working properly, it is also responsible for your thoughts, feelings and memory. It needs a constant supply of oxygen in the blood to work properly.

The spinal cord

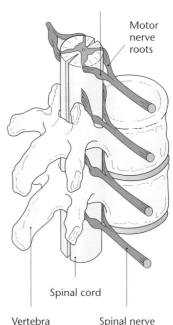

Sensory
nerve roots

Motor
nerve
roots

Spinal cord

Vertebra   Spinal nerve

The brain

Back   Front

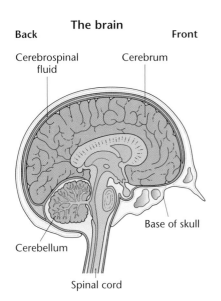

Cerebrospinal   Cerebrum
fluid

Base of skull

Cerebellum

Spinal cord

UNCONSCIOUSNESS

When the normal functions of the brain are interrupted, a casualty may become unconscious. Someone who is unconscious will not respond to you, even if you shout or pinch them.

If an unconscious person is lying on their back, their tongue may fall to the back of the throat and block their airway.

The table shows some of the main causes of unconsciousness:

CAUSE	EXAMPLES
Damage to brain	Head Injury
Blood not reaching the brain properly	Stroke
	Heart attack
	Fainting
Changes in content of blood reaching the brain	Shock
	Low blood sugar (hypoglycaemia)
	Poisoning, alcohol or drugs
Other conditions	Epilepsy

Whatever causes the unconsciousness, the three general rules of treatment are:
- keep the casualty's airway open;
- check and re-check the casualty's level of response; and
- examine the casualty thoroughly.

The recovery position keeps the airway open.

ASSESSING THE LEVEL OF RESPONSE

The casualty's level of response should be checked regularly. A casualty who is drowsy at first but then loses consciousness will probably need specialised treatment. A record of the casualty's levels of response will help the hospital or doctor treating them.

Remember the letters **AVPU**. This will help when you are making a quick assessment of the casualty's level of response.

Alert – how alert is the casualty?

Voice – does the casualty respond to your voice?

Pain – does the casualty respond to pain from, for instance, a pinch?

Unresponsive – does the casualty show no response?

A more detailed assessment can be made if you have time, using the table below:

EYES	MOVEMENT	SPEECH
Are they open?	Respond to commands?	Is it normal?
Do they open on command?	Move in response to pain?	Is it confused?
Do they respond to pain?	Make no response at all?	Can you understand what they are saying?
Do they stay closed?		Is there no response at all?

THE UNCONSCIOUS CASUALTY

The most important thing if someone is unconscious is to make sure their airway is clear and they are breathing. You should always suspect a neck or spine injury and take great care when moving the casualty.

An unconscious casualty's pulse rate will depend on the cause of their unconsciousness.

Don't!

- give an unconscious casualty anything to eat or drink;
- move the casualty unless you have to in case they have a spinal injury;
- leave the casualty alone.

Recognition

An unconscious casualty may:

- show no sign of being conscious;
- be breathing noisily.

Your aims are to

- keep the casualty's airway open;
- check and record the casualty's levels of response;
- treat any other injuries; and
- get the casualty to hospital urgently.

How you can help an unconscious casualty

- Follow the DRABC drill.
- Examine the casualty quickly, making sure their airway stays open.
- Treat any bleeding and support possible fractures.
- Put the casualty into the recovery position.
- Make a more detailed examination.
- If the casualty comes round within three minutes and is still well after 10 minutes, advise them to see a doctor.
- If the casualty does not come round within three minutes, phone 999 for an ambulance.
- Continue to check and record the casualty's breathing, pulse and level of response every 10 minutes. Make sure your records go with the casualty to the hospital.

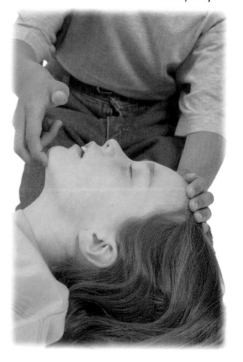

Make sure the casualty's airway is open.

HEAD INJURIES

All injuries to the head can be dangerous. Head injuries should always be seen by a doctor, especially if the casualty has been unconscious. The cause of unconsciousness may not be the head injury itself – the casualty could have been injured when they fell over.

The brain can be 'shaken' within the skull, by a blow to the head or jaw, or by a fall, which can cause unconsciousness for a short time.

Recognition

The casualty's history may reveal a blow or fall and the casualty also may:
- become unconscious for a short time;
- feel dizzy or sick;
- have a headache;
- not be able to remember what happened.

Your aims are to
- keep a check on the casualty until they are fully conscious; and
- get medical help if needed.

How you can help someone with concussion who is conscious and appears to be well
- Check the casualty's levels of response.
- If casualty is still well after 10 minutes and their level of response is satisfactory, advise them to see a doctor.

How you can help someone with concussion who is unconscious or becomes unconscious
- Follow the treatment for an unconscious casualty described in this chapter.
- Put the casualty in the recovery position (described in chapter 3) and phone 999 for an ambulance.
- Continue to check the casualty's breathing, pulse and levels of response.

SKULL FRACTURES

A direct force like a blow on the head can fracture the skull. Someone's skull can also be fractured by indirect force; for instance, falling from a height can fracture the skull even if the casualty lands on their feet. A direct blow may cause a depressed fracture, when bone is pushed in and damages the brain underneath. Fractures at the base of the skull are usually caused by indirect force such as that from falling heavily on the feet or the bottom (the base of the spine).

Recognition

The casualty's history may reveal a blow or fall and the casualty also may:
- show a drop in their level of response;
- become unconscious;
- have a wound, bruise or swelling on their head;
- have clear fluid or watery blood coming from their ears or nose; and
- have bloodshot eyes (may affect only one).

Your aims are to
- keep the casualty's airway open; and
- get the casualty to hospital.

How you can help a casualty who has a fractured skull
- Follow the DRABC drill.
- If the casualty is unconscious, follow the treatment for an unconscious casualty described above.
- If the casualty is conscious, help them to lie down (on a blanket, if possible) with their head and shoulders raised and supported.
- If there is bleeding or fluid coming from their ear, lean the casualty towards the affected side. Cover the ear with a sterile dressing or clean pad and secure it in place.

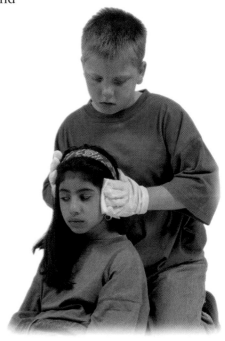

- Phone 999 for an ambulance.
- Look for and treat any other injuries.
- Check and record the casualty's breathing, pulse and levels of response every 10 minutes.

Handy hint!

Check for signs of injuries such as bleeding from the head, ears or nose, and for bruising around the eye. These signs may mean the casualty has a skull fracture. All casualties who have been unconscious (even for a short while) should be seen by a doctor.

COMPRESSION

A severe head injury or skull fracture may make the brain swell or lead to a build up of blood pressing on the brain. Such pressure on the brain is called compression. It can develop immediately or up to several days after a head injury. Compression can also be caused by a stroke or illness.

Recognition

The casualty's history may reveal a recent head injury or fall, the pupils of their eyes may be unequal or enlarged, and the casualty also may:

- show a drop in their level of response;
- become unconscious;
- have a wound, bruise or swelling on their head;
- be breathing noisily or their breathing may become slower;
- have a slow but strong pulse;
- have a headache;
- have a hot or flushed face;
- become grumpy or show other sorts of changes in their personality.

Your aims are to

- keep the casualty's airway open; and
- get the casualty to hospital as soon as possible

How you can help someone suffering from compression

- Phone 999 for an ambulance.
- Follow the treatment for an unconscious casualty.
- Check and record the casualty's breathing, pulse and levels of response every 10 minutes.

CONVULSIONS

A convulsion is also sometimes called a seizure or fit. It happens when the muscles in the body contract involuntarily. Convulsions are caused by a function of the brain being disturbed. This may be because of head injury, some poisons, a high temperature, or epilepsy.

EPILEPSY
Epilepsy is the name of a condition where the normal electrical impulses in the brain are disturbed. There are two types of epilepsy; minor and major.

Minor epilepsy
This may also be known as absence seizures. A minor epilepsy attack may go unnoticed because the casualty appears to be day-dreaming and may not realise what is happening.

Recognition
Someone who is having a minor epileptic seizure may:
- be staring and appear to be day-dreaming;
- be twitching their mouth, eyelids or head;
- be acting unusually, smacking or chewing their lips, for example;
- make strange noises or fiddle with their clothes.

Your aim is to
- protect the casualty from injury until they are fully recovered.

How you can help someone who is having a minor epileptic seizure
- Help the casualty to sit down in a quiet place, away from danger.
- Talk to them calmly to reassure them.
- Stay with the casualty until they are fully recovered.
- If the casualty is not known to have epilepsy, advise them to see a doctor as soon as possible.

A minor epileptic seizure needs calm reassurance.

Major epilepsy

These convulsions, often called 'tonic-clonic' seizures, can be quite dramatic. They can often be controlled by drugs.

Don't!

• try to hold the casualty during a convulsion;
• open their mouth or put anything in it

Recognition

The convulsions of someone who is having a major epileptic seizure often follow a pattern. The casualty may:

- have a strange feeling, taste or smell beforehand (known as an 'aura');
- become unconsciousness suddenly;
- go rigid, often arching their back, in the tonic phase of the seizure;
- make jerking movements in the clonic phase;
- have a rigid jaw;
- be frothing at mouth, possibly blood stained;
- be breathing noisily;
- wet themselves or have a bowel movement.

As the seizure passes, the casualty's muscles relax and their breathing becomes easier. The casualty then recovers but usually feels dazed. They may then fall asleep.

Your aims are to

- protect the casualty from injury; and
- stay with the casualty until they are fully recovered

Use something soft to protect the casualty's head.

How you can help someone who is having a major epileptic seizure

- If you are there when the seizure begins, try to protect the casualty from injury.
- Ask bystanders to keep clear.
- Loosen tight clothing around the casualty's neck and try to protect their head from getting knocked.

Handy hint!

As a casualty starts to recover, they can feel embarrassed, especially if they have wet themselves or had a bowel movement. Try to take them somewhere private to recover fully.

- When the convulsions stop, put the casualty into the recovery position.
- If the casualty goes into another seizure or continues convulsing without a break, call an ambulance.
- Stay with casualty until they recover fully or until an ambulance arrives.

CONVULSIONS IN CHILDREN

Convulsions in a young child are likely to be due to a high temperature rather than epilepsy. Children usually grow out of this type of convulsion.

Recognition

The casualty's history may show an illness, such a throat or ear infection, and the casualty also may:

- have hot flushed skin;
- be sweating;
- have twitching muscles;
- have 'rolled' or staring eyes;
- be holding their breath.

Your aims are to

- protect the child from injury;
- cool the child;
- reassure the parents; and
- get medical help.

Handy hint!

Remember, the child's parents will be worried and need plenty of reassurance. So don't 'take over' their child. Let mum or dad sponge the child if they want to help.

How you can help a child who is having convulsions

- Take off the child's clothes or bedcovers.
- Try to provide cool, fresh air but make sure the child doesn't get too cool.
- Place pillows so that any twitching will not injure the child.
- Sponge the child using barely-warm water.
- Put the child into the recovery position if possible.
- Phone 999 for an ambulance.
- Reassure the child's parents.

STROKE

A stroke happens when the blood supply to part of the brain is reduced, usually because one of the blood vessels which supply the brain becomes blocked or bursts. The effect of the stroke will depend on how much and which part of the brain is affected. Strokes are more common in elderly people and those with high blood pressure. The medical term for a stroke is cerebrovascular accident (CVA).

Recognition
The casualty may:
- show a drop in their level of response and be unable to speak;
- become unconscious, either suddenly or gradually;
- be confused or appear to be 'drunk';
- have a headache;
- show signs of weakness, usually on one side of their body only;
- be unable to speak.

Your aims are to
- keep the casualty's airway open; and
- get them to hospital.

How you can help someone who has had a stroke
- If the casualty is conscious, help them to lie down on a blanket with their head and shoulders slightly raised and supported.
- Lean the casualty's head to one side, and place a towel under their chin to soak up any dribble.
- Loosen any tight clothing.
- If the casualty is unconscious or becomes unconscious, follow the DRABC drill.
- Put the casualty into the recovery position and phone 999 for an ambulance.
- Check and record the casualty's breathing, pulse and level of response every 10 minutes.

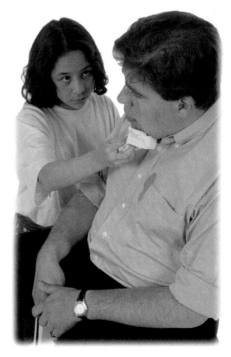

The casualty may dribble on the affected side.

DIABETES MELLITUS

This is a condition in which the body cannot control the amount of sugar (glucose) in the blood. The amount of sugar is controlled by a natural substance called insulin which is normally produced in the body by an organ called the pancreas.

If someone has diabetes, their pancreas either doesn't produce any insulin at all or doesn't produce enough to control the sugar levels properly.

Diabetes can be controlled by insulin injections, tablets or diet, depending on how severe the diabetes is. There are two conditions affecting diabetics which have very similar names: hyp**O**glycaemia and hyp**ER**glycaemia. Try to remember which is which.

These clues may indicate a casualty is diabetic.

HYPOGLYCAEMIA

Hypoglycaemia occurs when the level of sugar in the blood is lower than normal. The condition is usually found in known diabetics. For instance, a diabetic may have taken their insulin but missed breakfast. Some diabetics know when their level of sugar is dropping and will take extra sugar in the form of a high-sugar drink or sweets. It can also affect anyone who has not eaten for a while, particularly if they have taken strenuous exercise.

Recognition

The casualty may have a history of diabetes and also may:
- feel faint, confused or even aggressive;
- have pale and clammy skin and be sweating;
- have a strong, 'bounding' pulse;
- have shallow breathing;
- become unconscious.

Your aims are to
- raise the level of sugar if possible;
- stay with casualty until they are fully recovered; and
- get medical help if needed.

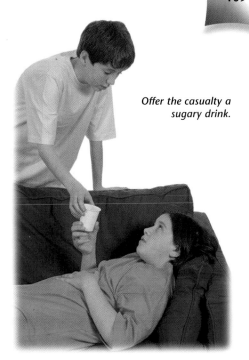

Offer the casualty a sugary drink.

How you can help someone with hypoglycaemia if they are conscious
- Help the casualty to sit down, and give them a sugary drink, sugar lumps, chocolate and so on.
- If their condition improves quickly, give them a little more to eat or drink, and allow them to rest until they are fully recovered.

How you can help someone with hypoglycaemia if they are unconscious
- Follow the DRABC drill.
- Treat the casualty as an unconscious casualty.
- Put the casualty into the recovery position.
- Phone 999 for an ambulance.

HYPERGLYCAEMIA

Hyperglycaemia happens when the level of sugar in the blood is higher than normal. The condition is often found in diabetics who have not yet been diagnosed and treated.

Although the effects of hypoglycaemia can affect people very quickly, hyperglycaemia usually takes days to develop.

Recognition

The casualty is usually unconscious and also may:
- be breathing deeply;
- have a fast pulse;
- have dry skin;
- sometimes have a smell of acetone (like nail varnish remover) on their breath.

Your aims are to
- keep the casualty's airway open; and
- get them to hospital.

How you can help someone with hyperglycaemia
- Follow the DRABC drill.
- Treat the casualty as an unconscious casualty (described earlier in this chapter).
- Phone 999 for an ambulance.
- Check and record the casualty's breathing, pulse and levels of response every 10 minutes.

Handy hint!

If the casualty is unconscious, you may not know they are diabetic. Look on their wrists for a medical alert bracelet and look in their pockets for a medical alert card, sugar lumps, glucose solution or an insulin syringe (the syringe may look like a pen).

A casualty suffering from hyperglycaemia is usually unconscious.

The effects of heat and cold

10

Our bodies work best at, or near to, a temperature of 37°C (98.6°F). A special centre in the brain is responsible for controlling this temperature and automatically adapts the body to hot or cold conditions.

In hot conditions – we sweat more and blood vessels near the skin get larger to enable more heat to be lost (when this happens we often look red in the face). The hairs on our skin lie flatter to let the sweat evaporate more easily and we breathe faster and deeper, taking in cool air to cool the blood as it passes through the lungs.

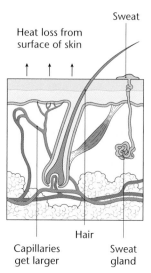

Sweat

Heat loss from surface of skin

Hair

Capillaries get larger

Sweat gland

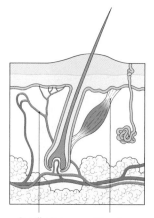

Capillaries get smaller

Muscles contract to erect hair

In cold conditions – we sweat less and blood vessels near the skin get smaller to keep warm blood in the main part of the body. The hairs on our skin rise up to trap warm air nearer the skin (when this happens it often shows as 'goose pimples'). We shiver, producing heat in the body tissues and we breathe slower and shallower, to stop heat loss from the blood as it passes through the lungs.

We can also control body temperature by our choice of clothing or by adjusting the heating or air conditioning.

Although the body is adaptable to changes in temperature, extreme heat or cold can still cause serious injury. Very young or elderly people are particularly at risk because they have more difficulty in adapting to temperature changes.

HYPOTHERMIA

Hypothermia is the name we give to the condition which develops when the body temperature drops to below 35°C. Low body temperature can result from being outdoors in cold conditions, particularly in wet and windy weather. It can also result from being in cold water.

People can be also be affected by hypothermia indoors if there is little or no heating. Elderly people and the very young are specially at risk.

Handy hint!

A fit young casualty can be warmed in a bath (40°C)if they are well enough to climb in without help.

Don't!

put a hot water bottle against the casualty's skin or let the casualty drink any alcohol – it will make things worse.

Recognition

The casualty's history may reveal exposure to cold. In severe cases, the casualty may suffer cardiac arrest. The casualty also may:
- show a drop in their level of response;
- become unconscious;
- have a slow pulse which is getting weaker;
- be shivering;
- have cold, pale, dry skin;
- behave unusually or be confused.

Your aims are to
- stop the casualty getting colder; and
- warm the casualty.

How you can help someone suffering the effects of cold indoors
- Replace any wet clothes with warm, dry ones.
- Put the casualty to bed and let them warm up gradually.
- Give the casualty warm drinks, and high-energy food, such as chocolate.

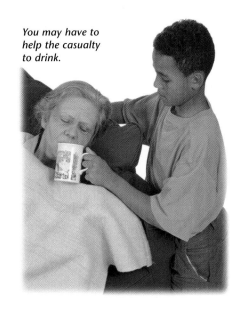

You may have to help the casualty to drink.

- if the casualty is an elderly person or a baby (or if you are in doubt about their condition) call a doctor.
- If the casualty becomes unconscious, follow the ABC of Resuscitation and phone 999 for an ambulance.

Handy hint!

Often the quickest, most effective way of warming up your casualty is to get in the sleeping bag with them to use your body heat. Always go out prepared with extra clothing, survival bags, high-energy food and drink and so on. Leave a route plan with someone responsible back at base.

How you can help someone suffering the effects of cold outdoors

- Protect the casualty from the cold with extra clothing, waterproofs or blankets. Remember to cover their head as well as their body.
- Take or carry the casualty to shelter as soon as possible.
- Protect the casualty from the ground and the weather by putting them in a dry sleeping bag, covering them with blankets or newspaper, and covering them again with a survival bag.
- Send for help. Try to send two people, as long as there is someone to stay with the casualty.
- If the casualty is conscious, give them hot drinks and high-energy food such as chocolate.
- If the casualty becomes unconscious, follow the ABC of Resuscitation.

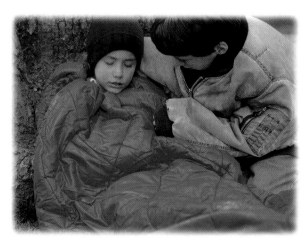

Don't!

put yourself at risk by wrapping the casualty in your own clothing.

Make sure you cover the head as well.

FROSTBITE

Frostbite happens when the tissues in the extremities freeze (for example, the fingers and toes). It is caused by exposure to cold, dry and windy weather conditions. Minor cases usually recover well but severe frostbite can cause permanent damage or the loss of the casualty's fingers or toes.

Warm gently without rubbing or chafing.

Don't! use direct heat, such as a hot water bottle, to warm the casualty or **rub the skin on the affected area as this can cause further damage.**

Recognition
The skin on the affected area may feel hard and it may turn white, then blue, then black. As the skin recovers, it becomes red, painful and hot. The casualty also may feel 'pins and needles' or numbness in the affected area.

Your aims are to
- warm the affected area slowly; and
- get medical help if needed.

How you can help someone suffering from frostbite
- Very gently take off their gloves, or boots.
- Warm the affected area gently in your hands, your lap or under the casualty's armpit.
- Get the casualty into warm shelter, carrying them (if possible) if their feet are affected.
- If the colour does not return to the skin quickly, put the affected area into warm water, then dry carefully and cover lightly with a dressing of dry gauze.
- Raise and support the affected limb to stop any swelling.
- Send the casualty to hospital, or suggest they see a doctor.

HEAT EXHAUSTION

Heat exhaustion develops slowly. It is caused by the loss of salt and water from the body through sweating. It particularly affects people who are not used to working or exercising in hot and humid conditions. It also affects people who are unwell, especially with vomiting and diarrhoea.

Recognition
The casualty may:
- be confused or dizzy;
- have a fast pulse which is getting weaker;
- have a headache;
- be sweating and have pale, clammy skin;
- suffer cramps in the limbs or abdomen;
- lose their appetite;
- feel sick;
- become unconscious in severe cases.

Your aims are
- to move the casualty to a cool place; and
- to replace lost fluid and salt.

How you can help someone suffering from heat exhaustion
- Help the casualty to lie down in a cool place.
- Raise and support their legs.

Raising the legs improves blood flow to the brain.

Handy hint!

If you are exercising on a particularly hot day, you should drink plenty of fluids and rest frequently.

- If the casualty is conscious, help them to sip plenty of water or weak salt solution (one teaspoon of salt dissolved in a litre of water).
- If the casualty recovers quickly, suggest they see a doctor.
- If the casualty becomes unconscious, follow the ABC of Resuscitation and phone 999 for an ambulance.
- Check and record the casualty's breathing, pulse and levels of response every 10 minutes.

HEATSTROKE

Heatstroke happens when the part of the brain which controls body temperature fails to do its job properly. This might be because the casualty is in very hot surroundings. It could also be caused by illnesses with a high fever, such as malaria.

Drugs like Ecstasy can also cause people to collapse from heatstroke because taking 'E' makes people very dehydrated as well as affecting their brain.

Heatstroke can come on suddenly, and the casualty may become unconscious very quickly.

Recognition
The casualty's history may reveal exposure to very hot conditions, illness or drug use and the casualty also may:
- show a rapid drop in their level of response;
- have a full, 'bounding' pulse;
- have a body temperature above 40C;
- complain of headache, dizziness and generally feel unwell;
- have hot, flushed, dry skin;
- become unconscious.

Your aims are to
- cool the casualty as soon as possible; and
- get medical help urgently.

How you can help someone suffering from heatstroke
- Help the casualty move to a cool place.
- Take off the casualty's outer clothing and wrap them in a cold, wet sheet. Keep wetting the sheet.
- Phone 999 for an ambulance.
- Continue cooling the casualty until their temperature drops to 38°C.

- Replace the wet sheet with a dry one and continue to keep a check on the casualty's temperature. If the temperature starts to rise again, repeat the cooling process.
- Fanning or sponging with cold water will help if there is no sheet available.
- If the casualty becomes unconscious, follow the ABC of Resuscitation.
- Check and record the casualty's breathing, pulse and levels of response every 10 minutes.

Keep the sheet wet by continually sprinkling water over it.

Handy hint!

If you are out clubbing or at a party or rave, you may see someone collapse suddenly with signs and symptoms of heatstroke. You should always suspect that drugs may be the cause and phone 999 for an ambulance.

Bones, joints and muscles

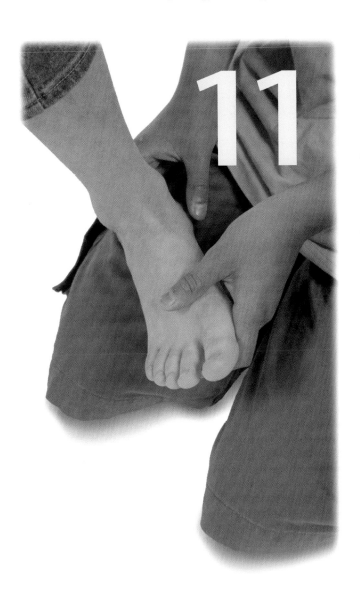

11

The skeleton is made up of about 200 separate bones. It supports the weight of our body and makes us the shape we are. It also protects important organs – for example, the ribs protect the heart and lungs and the skull protects the brain.

It also allows us to move by providing a framework to which muscles are attached.

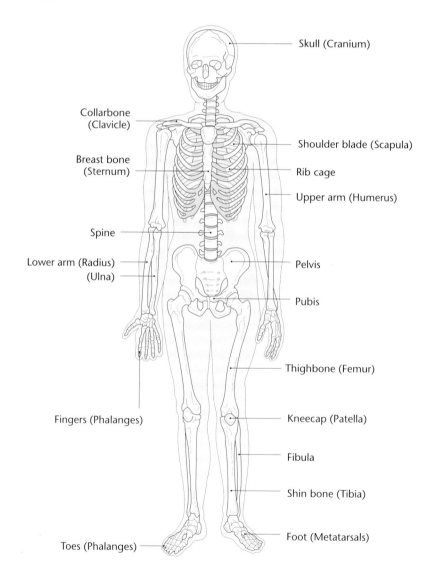

Skull (Cranium)

Collarbone (Clavicle)

Shoulder blade (Scapula)

Breast bone (Sternum)

Rib cage

Upper arm (Humerus)

Spine

Lower arm (Radius) (Ulna)

Pelvis

Pubis

Thighbone (Femur)

Fingers (Phalanges)

Kneecap (Patella)

Fibula

Shin bone (Tibia)

Foot (Metatarsals)

Toes (Phalanges)

JOINTS

Bones cannot bend, but wherever they meet, they form a joint, allowing us to bend, twist and turn. There are four main types of joint.

Hinge joints – can only move in one direction like a door hinge (examples are the knee and elbow).

Ball and socket joints – can move in a circular direction (examples are the shoulder and hip).

Slightly moveable joints – only allow slight movement (examples are the joints between the spine's vertebrae).

Fixed joints – are where the edges of bones fuse together and do not move (examples are the pelvis and skull).

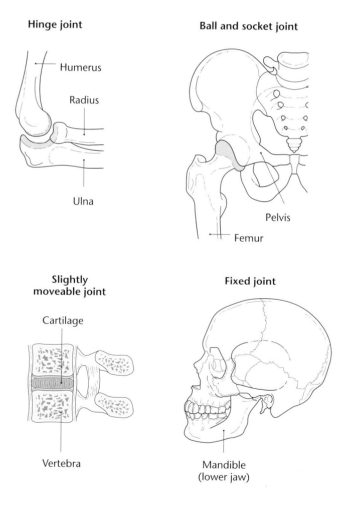

Hinge joint

Humerus

Radius

Ulna

Ball and socket joint

Pelvis

Femur

Slightly moveable joint

Cartilage

Vertebra

Fixed joint

Mandible (lower jaw)

MUSCLES

Muscles move your body. They are attached to your bones by tendons and work in pairs – one of the muscles contracts to bend the joint then the other one contracts to pull it back again as the first muscle relaxes. There are two types of muscle.

Involuntary muscles – work automatically without us thinking about them (examples are the heart muscle and muscles in the digestive system).

Voluntary muscles – are those we can control by thinking about them (examples are the muscles that move our arms and legs).

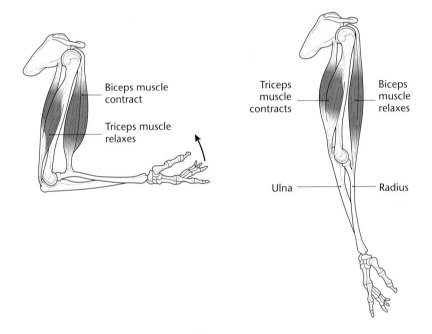

INJURIES TO BONES, JOINTS AND MUSCLES

There are various types of injury that affect bones, joints and muscles. We will look at these types in general before we turn to treating particular injuries.

FRACTURES

A fracture is a break or crack in a bone caused by direct or indirect force. In the case of **direct force** the bone breaks at the point of contact. As an example, someone's leg may be broken if they are hit by a car.

Indirect force breaks the bone at a place away from the point of contact. As an example, if someone falls heavily onto their hand, the force may be carried up their arm and break their collarbone.

There are three types of fracture.
Simple fracture – a clean break or crack.
Comminuted fracture – the bone breaks into little pieces.
Greenstick fracture – the bone bends but does not break completely. Greenstick fractures are common in young children.

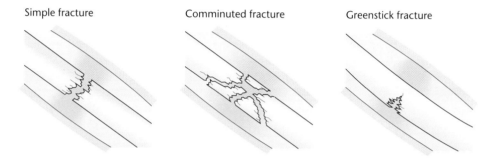

Simple fracture   Comminuted fracture   Greenstick fracture

There may be open wounds with all types of fracture and there may also be other injuries to muscles, nerves and organs. Fractures can be described as open or closed.
Open fracture – there will be a wound visible on the skin which may be caused by the force of the injury or by the bone itself breaking through the skin.
Closed fracture – the surrounding skin is not broken although there may be swelling.

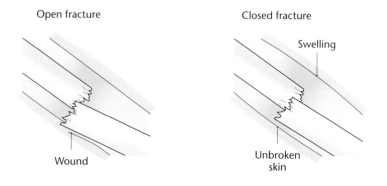

Open fracture   Closed fracture

Swelling

Wound

Unbroken skin

DISLOCATIONS

Bones can become dislocated at a joint if forced into an abnormal position. The most common joints affected are those at the shoulder, the thumb, the finger and the jaw. It can be difficult to decide whether an injury is a fracture or a dislocation. If you are not sure, *always* treat the injury as a fracture.

SOFT TISSUE INJURIES

These are injuries to the muscles and ligaments. They are commonly found in sports injuries. There are two main types.

Sprains – these are injuries to ligaments at or near a joint. Sprains can be caused by wrenching or twisting the joint, for instance during a fall.

Strains – these are injuries to a muscle and are sometimes called 'pulled muscles'. Strains can be caused by an awkward movement or a violent contraction of a muscle, for instance during sporting activity.

GENERAL TREATMENT FOR BONE, JOINT AND SOFT TISSUE INJURIES

Sometimes when you look at an injury, you see at once what has happened. For example, you may see an open fracture with the ends of the bone sticking out, or see a dislocated thumb.

Other injuries may only be properly diagnosed by an X-ray. If you are in doubt about the injury, *always* treat it as a fracture.

General recognition

The casualty's history may show a recent fall or a blow and there may have been the sound of the bone snapping. The bone or joint may simply 'not look right' and the casualty also may:

- have difficulty in moving a limb;
- feel pain at or near the injury which will feel worse when moving;
- have a wound at or near the injury which may be bleeding;
- have swelling and bruising;
- be suffering shock, particularly if injury involves the thighbone, ribs or pelvis.

Your general aims are to

- ease the swelling and pain; and
- get medical advice if needed.

CLOSED FRACTURES AND DISLOCATION

Your aims are to
- steady and support the injury; and
- get the casualty to hospital.

How you can help a casualty with a closed fracture or dislocation
- Try not to move the casualty more than you have to.
- Steady and support the injured part.
- If you have been trained to do so, provide firmer support with bandages.
- Arrange to get the casualty to hospital, depending on the injury.
- Treat the casualty for shock.
- Check and record the casualty's breathing and pulse every 10 minutes.
- Check every 10 minutes to make sure any bandages are not restricting the casualty's circulation.

OPEN FRACTURES

Your aims are to
- stop any bleeding;
- steady and support the injury; and
- get the casualty to hospital.

How you can help a casualty with an open fracture
- Try not to move the casualty more than you have to.
- Cover the wound with a pad or dressing and apply pressure to control the bleeding (see chapter 7)
- Raise the injured limb gently if possible.
- If the bone is sticking out, treat as a wound with an embedded object (see chapter 7), applying pressure **around** the object.
- Steady and support the injured part.

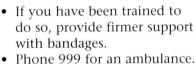

Handy hint!

Remember to protect yourself if the wound is bleeding. Use disposable gloves and keep sores and cuts covered with a plaster.

- If you have been trained to do so, provide firmer support with bandages.
- Phone 999 for an ambulance.
- Treat the casualty for shock.
- Check and record the casualty's breathing and pulse every 10 minutes.
- Check every 10 minutes to make sure any bandages are not restricting the casualty's circulation.

SOFT TISSUE INJURIES

As we have seen, a sprain is an injury to a ligament and a strain is an injury to a muscle. Sometimes, it is difficult to decide whether the injury is a sprain, strain or fracture – if you're not sure, treat it as a fracture.

Recognition

The casualty's history may show what caused the injury and the casualty also may:
- have difficulty in moving the joint;
- feel pain at or near the injury;
- have swelling and bruising.

Your aims are to
- ease swelling and pain; and
- get medical advice if needed.

How you can help someone with a soft tissue injury

Think of the word **RICE**. It will help you remember this procedure:

Rest, steady and support the injury.

Ice packs or cold compresses will cool the injured area to ease the swelling, bruising and pain.

Applying a cold compress to a sprained ankle.

Ho̦n̦d̦y̦ h̦i̦n̦ț!

A bag of frozen
peas is as good
as an ice pack in
an emergency.

*Support and bandage a
sprained ankle.*

Compression eases the swelling
and gives support so wrap the
area with a thick layer of
padding and bandage it
firmly.
Elevating the injury means
raising and supporting it.

Follow the **RICE** procedure then
advise the casualty to see a doctor
or visit a hospital.

FACIAL FRACTURES

Fractures on the face often affect the nose, cheekbones and jaw. They are
usually caused by a heavy blow, especially during a fight or a fall. The
main danger is that the casualty's airway may be blocked by swelling,
loose teeth or blood and saliva. There may also be head or neck injuries or
a fractured skull (see chapter **9**).

Your aims are to
- keep the casualty's airway open;
- check the casualty's breathing and pulse; and
- get the casualty to hospital.

How you can help someone with major facial injuries
- Follow the DRABC drill.
- Follow the general rules for treating fractures.
- Place the casualty into the recovery position. If the jaw is injured,
  place soft padding under the head to keep the weight off the jaw.
- Phone 999 for an ambulance.

How you can help someone with an injury to the lower jaw
- Help the casualty sit forward to allow any blood and saliva to drain away.
- Support the casualty's jaw with a soft pad.
- If the casualty is sick, continue to support their jaw and head and offer them water to rinse out the mouth.
- Get the casualty to hospital.

How you can help someone with a fractured cheekbone or nose
- Place a cold compress (see page **168**) against the injured area to ease the swelling.
- Treat bleeding from the nose if there is any (described in chapter **7**).
- Get the casualty to hospital.

BROKEN RIBS

Rib fractures are usually caused by a blow to, or a fall onto, the chest. Sometimes the broken rib goes into the lungs causing internal bleeding and difficulty with breathing.

Recognition
A casualty with broken ribs may:
- have shallow breathing;
- have difficulty breathing;
- feel sharp pain at the fracture which will be made worse by breathing;
- have a wound over the fracture which could allow you to hear air being sucked in;
- be coughing up bright red frothy blood;
- be suffering from shock.

Your aims are to
- support the casualty's chest;
- ease the casualty's breathing; and
- get the casualty to hospital.

How you can help someone with broken ribs
- Help the casualty to sit down. They may be most comfortable in a half-sitting position, leaning towards the injured side
- If there is a wound, treat it as a sucking chest wound (described in chapter **9**).
- Support the arm on the injured side in an elevation sling (described in chapter **15**)
- Phone 999 for an ambulance.
- Check and record the casualty's breathing and pulse every 10 minutes.
- If the casualty becomes unconscious, follow the ABC of Resuscitation.

Handy hint!

If there is no wound, the casualty may be more comfortable sitting up. Always ask the casualty to lean towards the injured side.

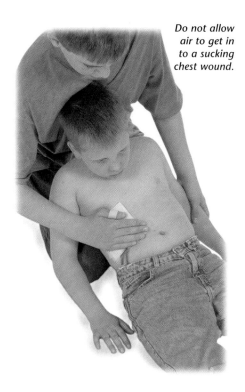

Do not allow air to get in to a sucking chest wound.

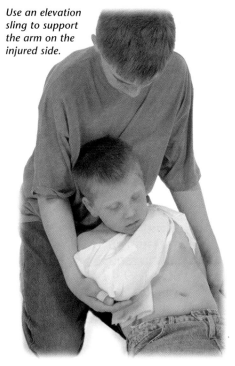

Use an elevation sling to support the arm on the injured side.

FRACTURED SPINE

The spine (including the neck) consists of many small bones linked by cartilage. Any of the bones may be fractured. The danger of an injury to the spine (or neck) is that the spinal cord may be damaged. This can lead to very serious permanent injury. If you think a casualty may have injured their back or neck, *always treat as a fractured spine.*

Recognition

The casualty's history may show a fall or other accident. When you are examining their spine, the casualty may complain of tenderness or you may feel a lump. The casualty also may:

- have difficulty breathing;
- feel pain in their back or neck;
- have no feeling or control of their limbs;
- feel tingling or 'pins and needles';
- have a 'heavy' or 'stiff' feeling in the limbs;
- be suffering from shock.

Your aims are to

- keep the casualty's airway open;
- check the casualty's breathing and pulse;
- prevent further injury;
- phone 999 for an ambulance.

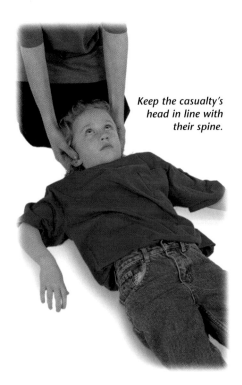

Keep the casualty's head in line with their spine.

How you can help someone with a fractured spine if they are conscious

- Reassure the casualty and ask them not to move.
- Steady and support the casualty's head in a neutral position by placing your hands over their ears.
- Phone 999 for an ambulance and tell ambulance control you suspect a spinal injury.

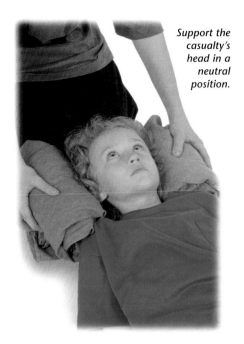

Support the casualty's head in a neutral position.

Don't!

move the casualty from the position you find them in, unless they are in danger, not breathing or unconscious.

How you can help someone with a fractured spine if they are unconscious
- Follow the ABC of Resuscitation, remembering an open airway must always come first.

If you need to turn the casualty onto their back to resuscitate them, you must keep the spine straight. This will take six people, one supporting the head and directing movement, while the others support the spine, working together.

Handy hint!

The casualty's history is important. Always check for a fractured spine if the casualty has been:
- injured after falling from a height;
- diving into a swimming pool;
- thrown off a horse or a motorbike;
- playing rugby; or
- in a road accident.

FRACTURED PELVIS

A fracture of the pelvis is usually caused by crushing or by a serious accident such as a car or train crash. The main danger is internal bleeding because of damage to organs such as the bladder.

Recognition
The casualty's history may show an accident. The casualty also may:
- be unable able to walk or stand;
- feel pain and tenderness around their hips made worse by moving;
- be unable to pass urine – if they do, it may be blood-stained and painful;
- be suffering from shock.

Pad and bandage the casualty's legs if you have been trained to do so.

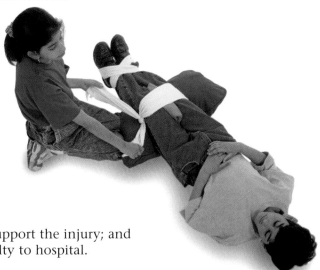

Your aims are to
- steady and support the injury; and
- get the casualty to hospital.

How you can help someone who has a fractured pelvis
- Help the casualty to lie on their back with their legs straight, or with their knees slightly bent and supported if that is more comfortable.
- Prevent the casualty's legs from moving by supporting on either side using items such as rolled up blankets, coats, boxes or bags.
- If you have been trained to do so, put padding between the casualty's legs, particularly their knees and ankles, and bandage their legs together (described in chapter **15**)
- Phone 999 for an ambulance.
- Treat the casualty for shock.
- Check and record the casualty's breathing and pulse every 10 minutes.

INJURIES TO UPPER LIMBS

The upper limbs are made up of the shoulders, collarbones, arms and hands. Injuries to the upper limbs are usually caused by blows or falls.

Recognition
The casualty's history may show an accident. The casualty also may:
- feel pain and tenderness which will be made worse by moving;
- be supporting the injured arm at the elbow;
- be leaning their head towards injured side.

Your aims are to
- steady and support the injury; and
- get the casualty to hospital.

Remember, you can use the casualty's jacket, belt or scarf to help support an injured arm.

How you can help someone with an injured upper limb
- Help the casualty to sit down.
- Steady and support the injury.
- If you are trained to do so, support the injured arm in a sling (described in chapter **15**) depending on the injury.
- Treat the casualty for shock.
- Get the casualty to hospital.

Injuries to the bones of the upper limbs are treated in slightly different ways as shown in the table below.

INJURY	PADDING	SLING	BROAD-FOLD BANDAGE
Collarbone	Between arm and chest	Elevation	Over sling
Shoulder	Between arm and chest	Arm	None
Upper arm and elbow that will bend	Between arm and chest	Arm	Over sling
Elbow that cannot bend	Between arm and body	None	Support in position found with broad-fold bandages around upper arm and chest, elbow and lower arm
Lower arm and wrist	Around arm	Arm	Over sling if required
Hand	Around hand	Elevation	Over sling if required

For injuries to the arm, use the arm sling and a broad-fold bandage to support.

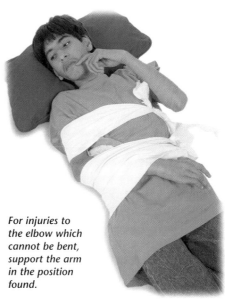

For injuries to the elbow which cannot be bent, support the arm in the position found.

For injuries to the hand, support in an elevation sling.

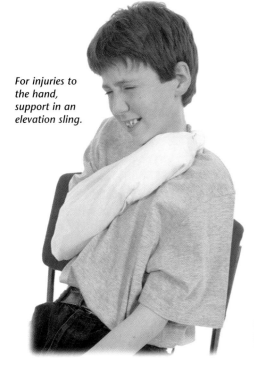

For injuries to the collarbone, use the elevation sling and a broad-fold bandage to support.

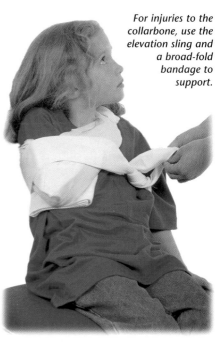

INJURIES TO LOWER LIMBS

The lower limbs include the hip joint, the thighbone, the knee, the lower leg, the ankle and the foot. Injuries to the lower limbs are usually caused by blows or falls or by road accidents.

Recognition

The casualty's history may show an accident. The injured leg may look shorter than the other or may be turned outwards. The casualty also may:

- feel pain and tenderness which will be made worse by moving;
- be unable to walk or have difficulty walking;
- be suffering from shock.

Your aims are to

- steady and support the injury; and
- get the casualty to hospital.

Handy hint!

Motorcyclists involved in a road accident often have a fractured thighbone. A lot of blood is lost internally into the muscles and tissues so the casualty suffers shock and must be sent to hospital urgently. Elderly ladies often break the top of the thighbone in falls because their bones break more easily as they get older. A shorter leg, which turns outwards at the knee and foot is a sign to look out for.

How you can help someone with an injured lower limb

- Help the casualty to lie down.
- Steady and support the injury.
- Straighten the leg by gently pulling the injured limb in the line of the bone.
- Prevent the casualty's legs from moving by supporting on either side using items such as rolled up blankets, coats, boxes or bags.
- Phone 999 for an ambulance.
- If you are trained to do so, support the legs with bandages (described in chapter 15).
- Treat the casualty for shock.
- Check and record the casualty's breathing and pulse every 10 minutes.
- Get the casualty to hospital.

Injuries to the bones of the lower limbs are treated in slightly different ways as shown in the table below.

INJURY	PADDING	SUPPORT
Pelvis	Between knees and ankles	Narrow-fold bandage to ankles. Broad-fold bandage around knees
Hip and thighbone	Between thighs, knees and ankles	Narrow-fold bandage around ankles Broad-fold bandages around knees, above and below fracture
Knee	Around joint	Support knee with pillow or folded blanket
Lower leg	Between knees, calves and ankles	Narrow-fold bandage around ankles Broad-fold bandage around knees, above and below fracture
Ankle	Between knees, calves and ankles	Narrow-fold bandage around toes Broad-fold bandage around knees and above ankle
Foot	Ice pack or cold compress	Raise and support only

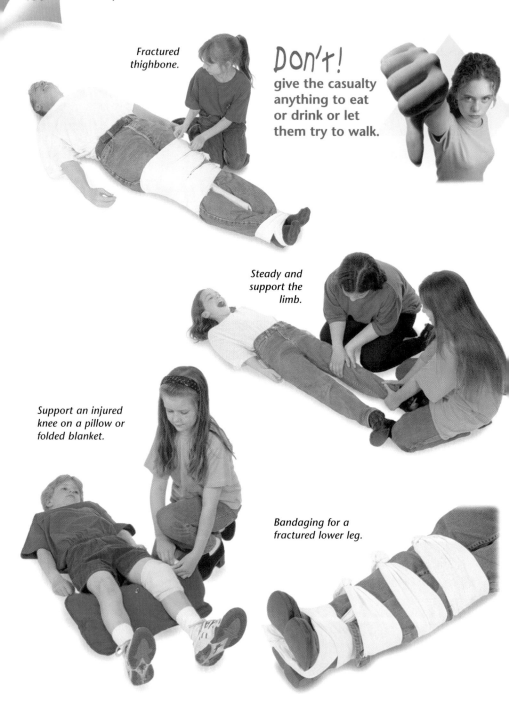

Fractured thighbone.

Don't!
give the casualty anything to eat or drink or let them try to walk.

Steady and support the limb.

Support an injured knee on a pillow or folded blanket.

Bandaging for a fractured lower leg.

CRAMP

Cramp is a sudden pain caused by a muscle tightening. It can be caused by exercise or can happen when you are asleep. Cramp usually affects the lower limbs.

A **stitch** is the name given to a similar pain in the muscles of the abdomen. A stitch can be eased by resting quietly.

Recognition
The casualty feels a sharp pain, usually in their thigh, calf or foot muscles.

Your aim is to
* help ease the pain.

How you can help someone with cramp
Foot – Help the casualty to stand with their weight on the front of the foot. Massage the foot.

Calf – Straighten the casualty's knee and push their foot firmly upwards towards the knee. Massage the affected muscles.

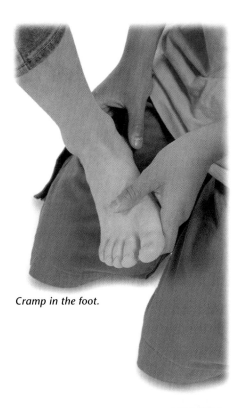

Cramp in the foot.

Cramp in the calf muscle.

Cramp in the thigh.

Thigh – Straighten the casualty's knee by raising the leg for cramp in the back of the thigh, or bend the knee for cramp in the front of the thigh. Massage the affected muscle.

Drugs and poisons

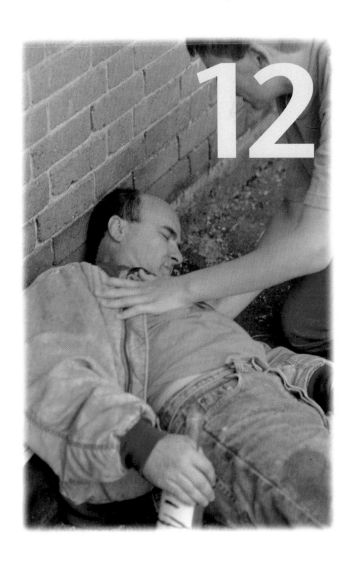

12

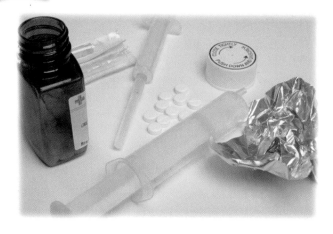

A poison is any substance which causes permanent or temporary damage when it enters the body. Some substances are helpful in small quantities but taking too much can be harmful. Paracetamol tablets, for example: they are taken to ease pain, but taking too many can cause liver damage.

Different poisons and drugs can be taken into the body in different ways.

Breathing – for example, gases and fumes, solvents and some glues, cannabis, tobacco smoke.

Swallowing – for example, alcohol, drugs in the form of tablets or medicine, poisonous plants such as some berries and mushrooms.

Injection – for example, drugs such as heroin, animal and insect bites and stings.

Absorption through the skin – for example, household and garden chemicals such as pesticides.

Once they are in the body, the poisons reach the blood and are carried to all parts of the body.

GENERAL RULES FOR TREATING POISONING
- Try to find out what the poison is and how much has been taken. Before they become unconscious, ask the casualty what they took.
- Check for clues around the casualty.
- Look on the labels of any containers you find.
- Check the casualty for the smell of alcohol or solvent on their breath, or for signs of blistering or burning on their lips or skin.
- When you phone for an ambulance, tell the control officer what you think the casualty has taken because the officer may be able to give you advice over the telephone before the ambulance arrives.
- If the casualty is sick, send a sample of vomit to hospital with them.

Whatever the poison, the basic treatment should be the same.

Your aims are to
- keep the casualty's airway open;
- check the casualty's breathing and pulse;
- identify the poison if possible; and
- get the casualty to hospital.

How you can help someone affected by poison or drugs if they are conscious
- Ask the casualty what happened.
- If the casualty is drowsy or losing consciousness, turn them into the recovery position.
- Check and record the casualty's breathing, pulse and level of response every 10 minutes.
- Get the casualty to hospital and make sure any containers, tablets, vomit or other clues go with them.

How you can help someone affected by poison or drugs if they are unconscious
- Follow the DRABC drill.
- Phone 999 for an ambulance.
- If the casualty is breathing, turn them into the recovery position.
- Check the casualty's breathing, pulse and levels of response every 10 minutes.

Don't!
try to make the casualty sick because it may do more damage.

ALCOHOL, DRUG AND SOLVENT ABUSE

Poisoning can be caused by any drug (including alcohol) whether it has been bought from a chemists' shop, prescribed by a doctor or taken illegally.

Mixing drugs (for instance, drinking alcohol and sniffing solvents) is particularly dangerous. The risk is even greater if the drug user has another condition such as diabetes, epilepsy or a heart problem.

Handy hint!

Remember to always check for other injuries – it is easy to miss a head or neck injury on a casualty who smells of alcohol. Keep the casualty warm – alcohol poisoning often causes hypothermia.

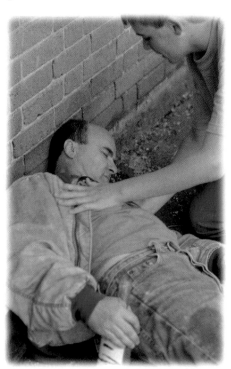

Always check for other injuries if a casualty has been drinking alcohol.

Recognition
Various drugs and poisons produce different signs and symptoms as shown in the table opposite.

Your aims are to
- keep the casualty's airway open;
- check the casualty's breathing and pulse; and
- get the casualty to hospital.

How you can help someone who has been poisoned by alcohol, drug or solvent abuse
Follow the general rules for treating poisoning.

Keep samples of vomit, empty containers, aerosol sprays, suicide notes or other clues and make sure they go with the casualty to hospital.

DRUG RECOGNITION

SOLVENTS Glue, aerosol sprays, lighter fuel	Headache, feeling sick, vomiting Hallucinations May be unconscious In severe cases, cardiac arrest
DEPRESSANTS Barbiturates, tranquillisers (an overdose is more likely if mixed with alcohol or other drugs)	Drowsy, may be unconscious Shallow breathing Weak, irregular pulse or very slow or very fast pulse (depends on the drug)
PAINKILLERS Such as aspirin and paracetamol (paracetamol has little effect at first)	May be unconscious, especially if mixed with alcohol or other drugs Pain, tenderness in upper abdomen Feeling sick, vomiting
STIMULANTS & **HALLUCINOGENS** Amphetamines ('whizz', 'speed'), LSD ('acid'), ecstasy ('E'), cocaine ('coke', 'charley'), crack	Excitable, wild behaviour Over-active Hallucinations Anxiety Confusion Sweating and shakiness, sickness and vomiting
NARCOTICS Heroin ('smack', 'H'), morphine	Drowsiness or unconsciousness Shallow breathing Pin-point pupils of eyes Sickness and vomiting Needle marks on arms or infection from sharing needles
ALCOHOL	Strong smell of alcohol Unconscious, may be rousable at first Deep, noisy breathing, becoming shallower Full, bounding pulse, becoming faster and weaker Flushed, sweaty face

HOUSEHOLD AND CHEMICAL POISONING

Every household contains poisons: these include bleach, paint stripper, glue, paraffin and weedkillers. They can be swallowed or, if spilled, can cause burns or be absorbed through the skin. *Always* keep dangerous chemicals locked away out of the reach of *young children*.

Handy hint!

Remember to protect yourself. Make sure there is no spilled chemical or open chemical container which could injure you.

Recognition

The casualty's history may show exposure to poisonous chemicals. The casualty also may:
- have problems with their airway and breathing and need resuscitating;
- have chemical burns or blisters on their lips and mouth;
- have burns on their skin from spilled chemicals.

Your aims are to
- keep the casualty's airway open;
- check the casualty's breathing and pulse;
- treat any chemical burns; and
- get the casualty to hospital.

Sips of water or milk may help.

Don't!
try to make the casualty sick as this can make the burning worse.

How you can help someone who has been poisoned by household or other chemicals
- Follow the general rules for poisoning and burns.
- If you need to give mouth-to-mouth ventilations, wash off the chemical around the casualty's mouth or use a face shield.
- If the casualty is conscious and has burns around their lips or mouth, give them frequent sips of water or milk.

POISONOUS PLANTS

Poisonous plants can be very dangerous if eaten. Young children are particularly at risk; they may be tempted to eat plants that have brightly coloured berries and seeds.

There are many different poisonous plants. Common ones include certain types of mushroom such as the death cap, the seeds of laburnum trees and lupins, daffodil and iris bulbs, and the berries from deadly nightshade, holly, laurel and yew.

Recognition
The casualty's history may show poisoning; for instance, you may have seen a child eating berries or seeds. The casualty also may:
- be unconscious;
- have been sick.

Your aims are to
- keep the casualty's airway open;
- check the casualty's breathing and pulse; and
- call a doctor or ambulance.

How you can help someone who has been poisoned by eating a plant
- Follow the general rules for poisoning.
- Decide whether to call a doctor or ambulance – if you are not sure, always phone 999 for an ambulance.
- Try to identify the plant and what part of it the casualty has eaten.
- Send pieces of the plant and any vomit to hospital with the casualty.

FOOD POISONING

Food poisoning is caused by eating food that has not been cooked properly or that has begun to 'go off'. It can take effect within two hours of eating or as long as 24 hours later, depending on what is wrong with the food.

Recognition
A casualty with food poisoning may:
- feel sick or vomit;
- have cramping pains in their abdomen;
- have diarrhoea;
- have a headache;
- suffer from shock and eventually collapse.

Your aims are to
- help the casualty to rest; and
- get medical help or advice.

How you can help someone with food poisoning
- Help the casualty to lie down and rest.
- Give the casualty plenty to drink, such as water or weak tea.
- Provide a bowl and damp flannel in case the casualty is sick.
- Decide whether to call a doctor or ambulance.
- If the casualty gets worse at any time, call an ambulance.

Handy hint!

Always suspect food poisoning if there is more than one casualty with the same problems. Mild attacks of food poisoning will often get better with rest and fluids. Always defrost and cook food properly. Never leave food lying around for a long time. Always make sure you wash your hands before handling food.

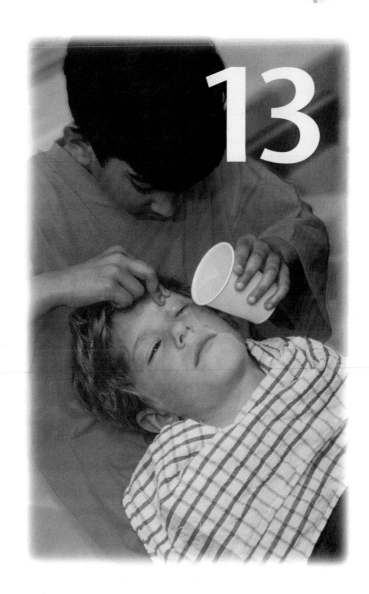

BITES AND STINGS

Unless they are scared, angry or injured, animals and insects don't usually attack people. Most attacks only cause discomfort but you should always look out for the signs of anaphylactic shock after someone has been bitten or stung.

BITES

Most bite injuries in Britain are from dogs or other people. Bites cause puncture wounds which can carry germs from the teeth and mouth deep into the casualty's skin, and this can lead to infections.

Recognition
The casualty's history may show the cause of the wound and the casualty also may:

- have bite marks on their skin which may have broken the surface;
- have redness and bleeding.

Your aims are to

- stop any bleeding;
- keep the wound clean; and
- get medical advice.

Handy hint!

Always remember your own safety if you are trying to rescue a casualty from an angry dog. Remember to protect yourself if the wound is bleeding. Use disposable gloves and keep sores and cuts covered with a plaster.

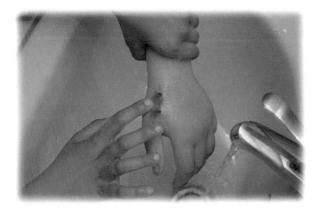

Wash the wound thoroughly with soap and warm water.

How you can help someone who has been bitten by an animal
- Wash the wound well with soap and warm water.
- Pat the wound dry and cover it with a plaster or small dressing.
- Advise the casualty to see a doctor about tetanus immunisation.
- For serious bites, treat bleeding then cover the wound with a clean or sterile dressing and send the casualty to hospital.

INSECT STINGS

Stings from bees, wasps and hornets are painful and frightening but they are not normally dangerous unless the sting is in the mouth or throat. Some people are allergic to stings and may develop anaphylactic shock (described in chapter 5).

Recognition
The casualty's history may show how the sting happened and the casualty also may:
- have felt a sudden sharp pain which has eased to tenderness;
- have redness or a mild swelling.

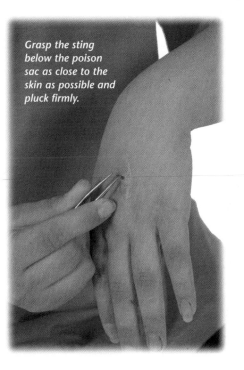

Grasp the sting below the poison sac as close to the skin as possible and pluck firmly.

Your aims are to
- ease the swelling and pain; and
- get the casualty to hospital if needed.

How you can help someone who has been stung by an insect
- If the sting is still there, remove it with tweezers.
- Put on a cold compress (described on page 168) to help to ease pain and swelling.
- Ask the casualty to see a doctor if the pain or swelling does not get better or if it gets worse during the next two or three days.
- If the casualty has been stung in the mouth, give them ice to suck and phone 999 for an ambulance.

OBJECTS IN THE EYE

Objects in the eye include things such as dust, grit or a loose eyelash. Most are easy to remove.

Recognition
A casualty with something in their eye may:

- have blurred vision;
- feel pain or irritation in their eye;
- have a red or watering eye.

Your aim is
- to prevent further injury to the casualty's eye.

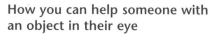

Don't!
touch anything stuck to, or embedded in, the eye or the coloured part of it.

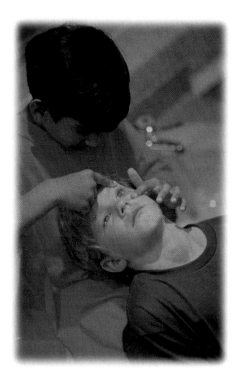

How you can help someone with an object in their eye
- Ask the casualty to sit down facing the light.
- Ask the casualty not to rub their eye.
- Gently separate the eyelids of the affected eye with your finger and thumb and look carefully at the eye.
- If you can see the object, wash it out using a glass or eye-wash and clean (preferably sterile) water.

Ask the casualty to look right, left, up, and down.

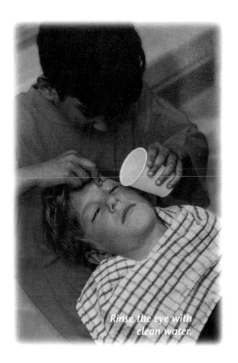

Rinse the eye with clean water.

- If this does not work, lift the object off the eye or eyelid with a moist swab, tissue or a clean handkerchief.
- If the object is stuck to the eye and can't be removed, cover the eye with an eyepad and send the casualty to hospital.

Handy hint!

Even after the object has been removed from the eye, the eye will continue to feel sore for a while.

OBJECTS IN THE EAR

Young children often push small objects into their ear. These can become stuck and may cause deafness. Sometimes, an insect flies or crawls into the ear and may cause a similar problem.

Don't!

try to remove an object that is stuck in someone's ear – you may push it further in.

Recognition

The casualty's history may show that something has got into their ear. The casualty also may:

- be unable to hear in the affected ear;
- if it is an insect, the casualty may complain of a buzzing sound or feel movement in their ear.

Your aim is to

- prevent further injury to the casualty's ear.

Support the head with the affected ear uppermost.

How you can help someone with an object in their ear
- If you think that it is an insect, ask the casualty to sit down and gently pour warm water into their ear so that the insect floats out.
- If this does not work or if any other object is stuck in the ear, the casualty should be sent to hospital.

HEADACHES

A cold compress may help a headache.

A headache can be anything from a continuous ache to a severe 'blinding' pain. Headaches are often caused by tiredness, stress or worry but also happen with illnesses such as flu.

Headaches may also indicate more serious conditions such as meningitis, strokes or head injuries.

Recognition
The casualty may:
- feel an ache or pain in their head;
- be dizzy;
- feel sick.

Your aims are to:
- ease the pain; and
- get medical advice if needed.

How you can help someone with a headache

- Help the casualty to sit or lie down in a quiet place.
- If possible, try to get rid of possible causes of the headache such as loud noises, bright lights and cigarette smoke.
- If the pain does not get better within two hours, or if you are worried, call a doctor.
- An adult may take their own painkillers if they wish, such as two paracetamol tablets.

Handy hint!

Always call a doctor if the casualty has:
- severe headache which comes on suddenly;
- severe pain which carries on for more than two hours;
- a drop in the level of response;
- a headache with a stiff neck;
- a headache following a head injury.

EARACHE

Earache is most common in children and is normally due to an infection. People also get earache with a cold or flu, or after air travel.

Recognition

The casualty's history may show a cold or flu, or air travel. The casualty also may:
- feel a throbbing pain in their ear;
- have a 'dirty' coloured discharge coming from the ear;
- have difficulty hearing.

Your aims are to
- ease the pain; and
- get medical advice if needed.

Rest the affected ear against something warm.

How you can help some who has an earache
- Ask the casualty to hold something warm, such as a covered hot water bottle, against the affected ear.
- If there is a discharge from the casualty's ear, if they have a high temperature or if you are worried, get medical advice.
- An adult may take their own painkillers if they wish, such as two paracetamol tablets.

TOOTHACHE

Toothache is usually caused by a decaying tooth. It is sometimes made worse by hot or cold food or drinks.

Recognition
The casualty will certainly know if they have toothache! They will complain about a throbbing pain in the tooth. Their history may show a bad tooth and they also may:
- have swollen gums around the tooth;
- have bad breath.

Your aims are to:
- ease the pain; and
- encourage the casualty to visit a dentist.

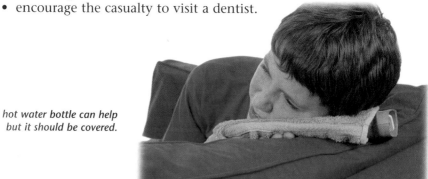

A hot water bottle can help but it should be covered.

How you can help someone with toothache
- Advise the casualty to hold a covered hot water bottle against their face.
- Encourage them to visit a dentist.
- An adult may take their own painkillers if they wish, such as two paracetamol tablets.

BACKACHE

Aches in the back and neck are often caused by lifting and bending badly. A fall can also cause ache or pain in the back.

A pain in the neck may be caused by 'whiplash' in a car crash.

Recognition
The casualty's history may show a fall or other accident. The casualty also may:
- feel pain in their back or neck which may be made worse by moving;
- feel pain going down their arms and legs; or
- have 'pins and needles' or tingling in their arms and legs.

Handy hint!

If the pain in the back or neck has been caused by a fall or a blow, it should always be treated as a possible fractured spine (described on page 130)

Your aims are to
- ease the pain; and
- get medical advice if needed.

How you can help someone with backache
- Help the casualty to lie down in the most comfortable position on a firm surface.
- Advise the casualty to rest until the pain eases.
- Ask the casualty to see a doctor.
- If the casualty is in severe pain or if you are worried, seek medical advice.
- An adult may take their own painkillers if they wish, such as two paracetamol tablets.

Help the casualty to lie down in a comfortable position.

SORE THROAT

Most sore throats are due to an infection, cold or flu. A sudden pain in the throat when eating may be due to a piece of food becoming stuck and should be treated as choking (described in chapter 5).

Recognition
The casualty's history may show a cold, flu or cough and the casualty may complain of pain in their throat, made worse when swallowing.

Your aims are to
- ease the pain; and
- get medical advice if needed.

How you can help someone with a sore throat
Check the casualty's history carefully.
- An adult may take their own painkillers if they wish, such as two paracetamol tablets.
- If the pain does not improve, suggest the casualty sees a doctor.

Don't!
give painkillers to children – it is up to their parents or another responsible adult to take that decision, although you can suggest painkillers may be helpful. Children under 12 years should never be given aspirin.

ABDOMINAL PAIN

Pain in the abdomen can be due to indigestion, a stitch (described in chapter 11), food poisoning (described in chapter 12) or to conditions such as appendicitis. Mild pain will normally ease but if it gets worse or doesn't ease, the casualty should always see a doctor.

Recognition
The casualty may:
- feel ache or pain;
- have wind;
- feel sick or vomit.

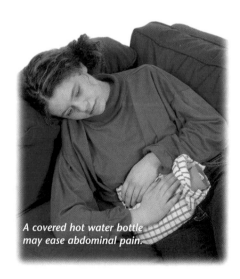
A covered hot water bottle may ease abdominal pain.

Your aims are to:
- ease the pain; and
- get medical advice if needed.

How you can help someone with abdominal pain
- Make the casualty comfortable and provide a bowl and damp cloth in case they are sick.
- Give the casualty a covered hot water bottle to put against their abdomen.
- If the pain is severe or doesn't ease after 30 minutes, call a doctor.

Handy hint!

Abdominal pain in teenage girls and adult women may be due to the start of their period. A mild painkiller (such as paracetamol) may help.

DIARRHOEA AND VOMITING

Diarrhoea and vomiting is usually caused by food poisoning or a 'bug'. People may have diarrhoea without vomiting or vomiting without diarrhoea – but when they have both, there is a greater risk of dehydration because of loss of fluids.

Handy hint!

Babies and young children can lose fluids very quickly. Always call the doctor if you are worried.

Your aim is to:
- encourage the casualty to keep taking fluids.

How you can help someone suffering from diarrhoea and vomiting
- Give the casualty plenty to drink – water, diluted fruit juice or weak tea.
- Reassure the casualty if they are being sick.
- Advise the casualty not to eat for about 24 hours.
- If the vomiting and diarrhoea continue, seek medical advice.

Emergency childbirth

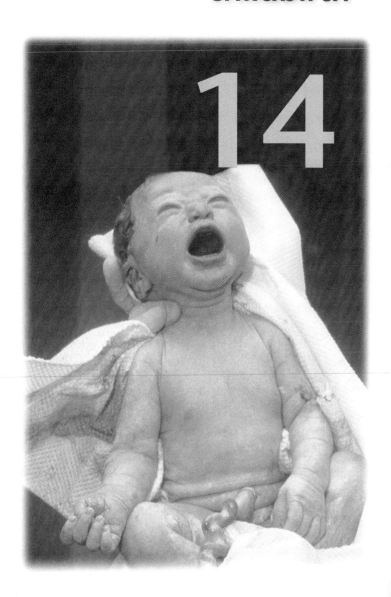

14

As a first aider, you may be with a mum-to-be – perhaps your own mother, your sister, a relative or a friend – when she starts to have her baby. We call the process of having a baby 'labour'. If a mum-to-be 'goes into labour' when you are with her, you may have to help.

Labour normally lasts several hours so there is usually plenty of time for the mum-to-be to get to hospital or for help (usually a midwife or a doctor) to arrive at home, depending on where the baby is going to be born.

Your aim is to
- get the mum-to-be to hospital or to get trained help to her.

Handy hint!

How you can help if a mum-to-be goes into labour
- Make the mum-to-be comfortable and stay with her.
- Phone the hospital or midwife (ask the mum-to-be if she has the number written down somewhere) or phone 999 for an ambulance.
- Help the mum-to-be to contact her husband, partner or other relative.
- Help her to pack a bag if she is going to hospital, make her a cup of tea, and try to keep any other children busy by playing with them.
- If either of you are worried, phone 999 and speak to the ambulance control officer. The officer will be able to give you advice over the telephone.

Don't panic – babies are seldom born before a doctor, midwife or ambulance arrives.

Help the mum-to-be to get comfortable.

First aid kits, dressings and bandages

15

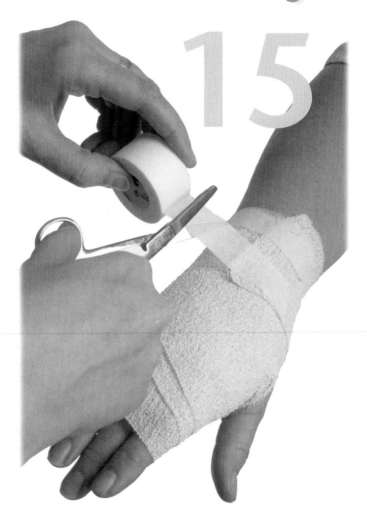

So far we have looked at how you, as a first aider, may be able to help if you have to treat particular injuries or illnesses. Now, this chapter tells you more about first aid kits, dressings and bandages.

FIRST AID KITS

There should be a first aid kit at home, in the car and at school. At home, many people keep first aid kits in the bathroom but they should really be stored in a dry place.

Places where people work have strict guidelines to follow, and their first aid kits must contain certain items, depending on the situation.

A good first aid kit should include the following items:
- 20 adhesive dressings (plasters);
- 6 medium sterile dressings;
- 2 large sterile dressings;
- 2 extra-large sterile dressings;
- 2 sterile eye pads;
- 6 triangular bandages;
- 2 roller bandages;
- 6 safety pins;
- disposable sterile gloves;
- a notebook and pencil; and
- a face shield (to be used only if you have been trained to do so).

A first aider might want to add tweezers and scissors to this list. Extra dressings and bandages are always useful, too.

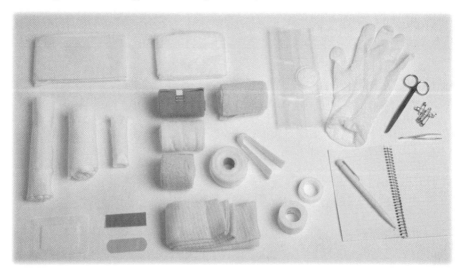

Don't!
**put anything
in a first aid kit
if you don't know
how to use it.**

If the first aid kit is to be taken on a camping trip or to an outdoor activity, it might also include:
- a torch;
- a whistle;
- extra triangular bandages;
- blankets; and
- a survival bag.

Dressings and Bandages

Dressings and bandages are not the same thing.

A **dressing** is used to cover a wound to protect it from further injury and help prevent infection.

A **bandage** is used to:
- keep direct pressure over a dressing;
- keep dressings and splints in place;
- help keep an injury still;
- support a limb or joint.

DRESSINGS

Dressings cover wounds, protect against infection and help to stop bleeding. Always try to use a pre-packed sterile dressing if possible. If a proper sterile dressing is not available, use clean non-fluffy material instead, such as a triangular bandage, a clean handkerchief, a tea-towel or a pillow case.

When using dressings
- always explain to the casualty what you are going to do;
- use a dressing big enough to cover the wound completely;
- put the dressing directly onto the wound – do not slide it into place;
- do not remove a dressing if the wound is bleeding through it – taking it off might disturb the blood clot forming underneath, so just put another dressing on top of the first one;
- wear disposable protective gloves if possible;
- try not to touch the part of the dressing which will touch the wound; and
- do not talk, sneeze or cough over the wound.

STERILE DRESSINGS

These are also sometimes called 'ambulance dressings'. They are made of a dressing pad attached to a roller bandage and come in various sizes.

Sterile dressings are packed individually and sealed by a protective wrapping. If the seal on the wrapping has been broken, the dressing will no longer be sterile.

Handy hint!

Remember to protect yourself if a casualty's wound is bleeding. Use the disposable sterile gloves from the first aid kit and keep sores and cuts covered with a plaster.

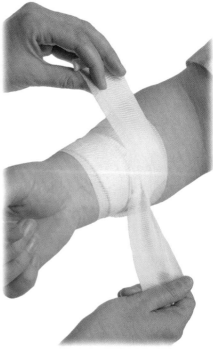

How to apply a sterile dressing

- decide which is the best size of dressing – if only one size is available, you will have to do your best with that;
- take off the wrapping and carefully unwind the loose end of the bandage;
- unfold the sterile pad, trying not to touch it;
- holding the bandage on either side of the pad, put the dressing directly onto the wound;

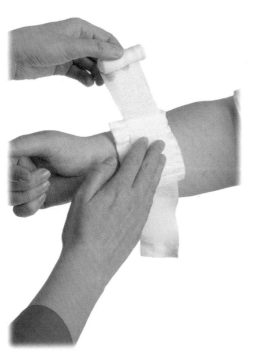

- wrap the shorter end of the bandage around the limb and dressing once to hold in place, then wind the other end around the limb, coming above and below, either side of the short end until the pad is covered;
- tie the ends in a reef knot (described later in this chapter), tying the knot over the pad to put firm pressure on the wound;
- if bleeding comes through the dressing, do not remove it but put another one on top;
- check the casualty's circulation is not restricted by the dressing.

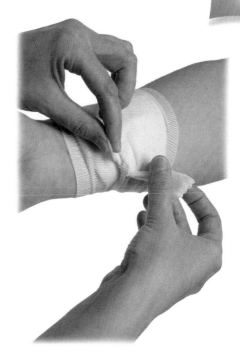

OTHER DRESSINGS

If a proper sterile dressing is not available, any clean non-fluffy material can be used. This could be a gauze pad, a triangular bandage or a clean handkerchief or tea-towel.

How to apply other dressings

- put a pad of clean material onto the wound; and
- hold the pad in place with a roller bandage, triangular bandage or pieces of cloth secured with adhesive strapping.

ADHESIVE DRESSINGS

Adhesive dressings are usually called 'plasters'. They are made of a small dressing pad attached to adhesive backing. The backing may be made of fabric, of waterproof or of non-allergenic material. Plasters are useful for small wounds and come in all shapes and sizes.

How to apply an adhesive dressing

- ask the casualty if they are allergic to plasters;
- decide which is the best size and shape to use;
- take off the wrapping and hold the plaster, pad side down, by its protective strips;

- peel back, but do not remove, the protective strips then put the dressing pad onto the wound; and
- carefully remove the protective strips, pressing down the edges and ends.

COLD COMPRESS

The swelling and pain of injuries such as bruises or sprains can be eased by cooling the injured area. This can be done by putting it under cold running water or soaking it in a bowl.

Sometimes, it may be easier to use a cold compress. There are two types:
- an ice-bag wrapped in cloth; and
- a pad soaked in cold water.

How to use an icepack
- half-fill a plastic bag with small ice cubes or crushed ice and knot the top;
- wrap the bag in a piece of cloth, such as a triangular bandage or teatowel, and put it on the injury, using a roller bandage to hold in place if needed.

How to use a cold pad
- soak a flannel or towel in very cold water then wring it out;
- put it on the injury; and
- cool the injury for about 20 minutes, keep the pad cold by re-soaking it frequently.

BANDAGES

There are three main types of bandage.

Triangular bandages – are usually made of cloth (although disposable paper versions are available) and used as slings to keep dressings in place and help to immobilise injured limbs.

Roller bandages – are used to keep dressings in place and support limbs

Tubular bandages – are used to keep dressings on, especially fingers and toes, or to support joints.

TYING BANDAGES – THE REEF KNOT

A reef knot should always be used to tie a bandage. The reef knot is very easy to tie, will lie flat, is comfortable for the casualty, and won't slip.

How to tie a reef knot

1 Pass the left end over the right, and under.

2 Bringing both ends up again, pass the right end over the left and under.

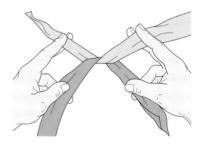

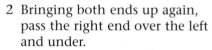

3 Pull the ends firmly, tightening the knot.

4 Tuck the ends underneath.

How to untie a reef knot
- Pull one end and one piece of bandage apart.
- Holding the knot, pull the end straight through and out.

When using bandages
- always explain to the casualty what you are going to do;
- make the casualty as comfortable as possible;
- keep the injured part supported – ask the casualty to help do this if possible;
- always work in front of the casualty, from the injured side if possible;
- if the casualty is lying down, pass the bandages under the body, using the natural hollows at the neck, small of back, knees and ankles – slide the bandages into place by easing them from side to side;
- put the bandage on firmly enough to control bleeding or hold a dressing but *not* so tightly that it will restrict the casualty's circulation;
- if possible, leave the casualty's fingers or toes uncovered so you can check their circulation after bandaging;
- always use a reef knot, tucking the ends in, but try not to tie the knot over a bony area;
- use padding, such as towels or clothing, between the casualty's limb and their body or between their legs, especially around the joints;
- tie the knot at the front of the body on the uninjured side if you are trying to immobilise a limb – if both sides of the body are injured, tie the knot in the middle;
- check every 10 minutes that the casualty's circulation is not restricted by a bandage .

CHECKING CIRCULATION

If you bandage a casualty's limb, you must always check that their circulation has not been restricted. Check this immediately after bandaging the limb and then check again every 10 minutes. Limbs often swell after an injury so although a bandage may not have been too tight when you put it on, it may become tighter as the limb swells causing it to restrict the casualty's circulation.

Recognition
If a bandage is too tight, the skin on the casualty's hand or foot may feel cold. Later it may turn a grey or blue-ish colour. The casualty also may:
- feel tingling or numbness;
- not be able to move the affected part.

How to check for restricted circulation

To check that a bandage is not restricting the circulation:
- press the skin of the casualty's hand or foot, or one of their finger or toe nails, until it is pale;
- release the pressure and the colour should return immediately;
- if the skin or nail remains pale, the bandage is too tight.

Loosen a tight bandage by unrolling or undoing just enough of it for warmth and colour to return then reapply the bandage.

ROLLER BANDAGES

There are three main types of roller bandages.

Open weave – are used to keep small dressings in place. Because of the loose-weave, these cannot be used to apply pressure or give support.

Conforming – are used to keep dressings in place, and provide light support to injuries.

Crepe – are used to give firm support, especially to joints.

When using roller bandages
- always explain to the casualty what you are going to do;
- make the casualty as comfortable as possible;
- always make sure you use the right size – it is better to be too wide than too narrow;
- when a roller bandage is partly unrolled, the roll is called the 'head' and the unrolled part the 'tail' – always keep the head uppermost when bandaging and don't unroll too much at a time;
- work from in front of the casualty, supporting the injured part in the position you want it to be after bandaging;
- put the tail on the limb, and make two straight turns with the head to keep in place, working from inside to out;
- continue making turns with the bandage;

- check the casualty's circulation before you secure the bandage;
- secure the bandage with adhesive tape, safety pins, or by tucking it in.

How to use a roller bandage on an arm or leg
- Put the tail of the bandage round the wrist or lower leg, and working inside to out, make two straight turns with the bandage's head.
- Continue working up the limb, covering between half and two-thirds of the bandage on each turn.
- Finish off with a straight turn and secure.
- Check the casualty's circulation.

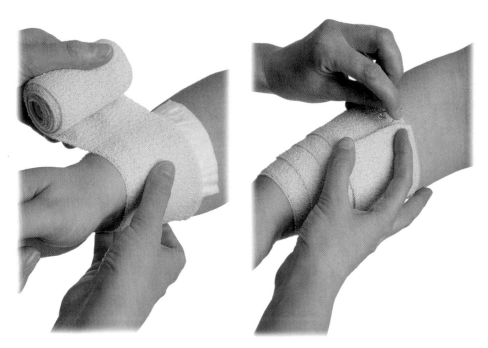

How to use a roller bandage on a hand or foot
Roller bandages may be used to keep dressings in place or to provide support to an injured wrist or ankle. If used for support, make sure the bandage extends well beyond the joint. The same method can be used for a hand or foot.
- Supporting the arm, place the tail on the inside of the wrist at the base of the thumb and make two turns.

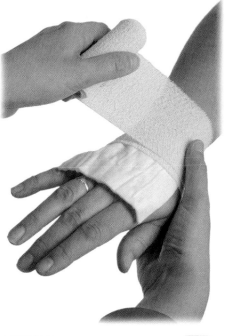

- Bring the bandage diagonally across the back of the hand, then take it under and around the fingers twice so that the edge of the bandage is against the base of the nail of the little finger.
- Bring the bandage diagonally back across the back of the hand and round the wrist.
- Continue working in this figure-of-eight, covering three-quarters of the previous turn each time.
- Leave the thumb free.
- Once the hand is covered, make two straight turns round the wrist and secure.
- Check the casualty's circulation regularly.

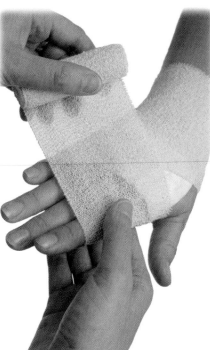

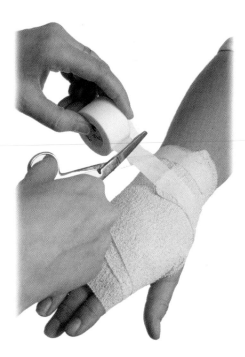

How to use a roller bandage on an elbow or knee

Roller bandages are much better than triangular bandages for keeping dressings in place at elbows and knees. The same method can be used for an elbow or knee.

- Support the arm in a bent position if possible.
- Try not to bandage with the arm straight because the casualty will then be unable to bend their arm after the bandage is on.
- Put the tail on the inside of the elbow and pass the bandage under and around to hold the bandage in place.
- Make one turn above the elbow covering half the bandage from the first turn.
- Cross over and make another turn, this time below the elbow and covering half of the first straight turn.
- Continue bandaging, one above, one below, covering between half and two-thirds of the previous layer each turn.
- Make two straight turns to finish and secure.
- Check the casualty's circulation regularly.

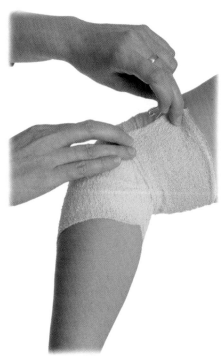

TUBULAR GAUZE

This is a tubular bandage made from a tube of seamless gauze. Tubular gauze comes in a variety of sizes and is very useful for keeping small dressings on fingers and toes. It is put on with the special applicator provided with the roll when it is bought.

How to use tubular gauze

- Cut a piece of tubular gauze $2\frac{1}{2}$ times the length of the finger, and push the whole length onto the applicator.
- Gently slide the applicator over the finger and dressing.
- Hold the end of the tubular gauze down at the base of the finger, and gently pull the applicator away until the finger has been covered with a layer of gauze.
- Twist the applicator twice, slightly away from the fingertip to prevent pinching it, then gently push the applicator back over the finger until it is covered with a second layer.
- Remove the applicator.
- Secure the bandage in place with adhesive tape.

TRIANGULAR BANDAGES

Triangular bandages are sold in single sterile packs and are usually made of linen or calico (although a disposable paper type is also available). Triangular bandages have several uses, including:

- open as slings or to secure a hand, foot or scalp dressing;
- unopened as a sterile pad on wounds to stop bleeding;
- folded into a broad-fold bandage to support and immobilise limbs and to secure splints and bulky dressings; or
- folded into a narrow-fold bandage to immobilise feet and ankles and to secure dressings to limbs.

Folding a triangular bandage
- Open out the bandage and lay it flat.

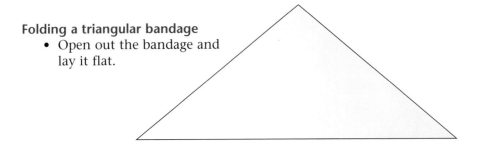

- Bring the point of the bandage up to the long straight side (the base).

- A broad fold bandage can be made by folding the bandage again.

- Folding again will make a
  narrow-fold bandage.

How to store triangular bandages

If the bandage has been opened but not used, it is no longer sterile.
However, it can still be used if a sterile bandage is not needed, for instance
as a sling or to immobilise fractures.

Bandages to be stored should be folded like this:
- Fold the bandage into a narrow-fold bandage.
- Bring the two ends into the centre.

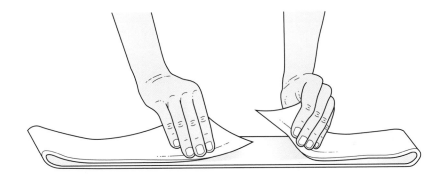

- Fold the ends into the centre
  again until a convenient size
  is reached.
- Always store bandages in a
  clean dry container such as a
  clean ice-cream tub with lid
  or a biscuit tin.

SLINGS

There are two different types of sling.

Arm sling – used to support injuries to the arm or wrist or used to relieve the weight from a dislocated shoulder.

Elevation sling – used to support the arm if the collarbone or shoulder is injured or used for hand injuries because it helps to control bleeding and reduce swelling.

How to apply an arm sling

- Support the casualty's arm with their hand slightly higher than the elbow.
- Put the bandage between the arm and chest, pulling one end up around the back of the neck to the injured side. The base should be level with the little finger nail.
- Bring the other end of the bandage up over the arm to meet the other end at the shoulder.

- Tie a reef knot in the hollow over the collarbone on the injured side, tucking the ends underneath.
- Bring the point to the front of the elbow, tucking loose bandage underneath and secure with a safety pin.
- Check the casualty's circulation and adjust the sling if needed.

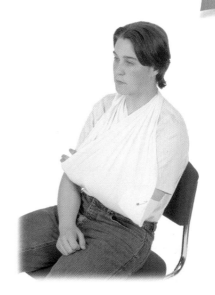

How to apply an elevation sling

- Put the casualty's arm on the injured side across their chest, with the fingertips touching the opposite shoulder.
- Put the bandage over the arm, with the point to the elbow and one end over the shoulder.

 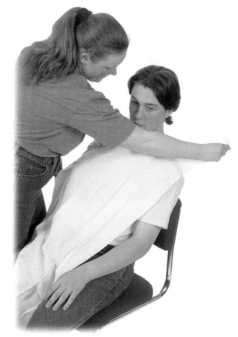

- Support the arm and tuck the base under the forearm and behind the elbow.
- Bring the lower end diagonally across the back to meet the other end at the shoulder.
- Secure with a reef knot in the hollow above the collar bone and tuck the ends in.
- Fold the point forward, tucking in any loose bandage, and secure with a safety pin.
- Check the casualty's circulation and adjust the sling if needed.

Makeshift slings

If you don't have a proper triangular bandage, you can make a sling from a square of cloth but make sure it is strong enough to take the weight of the arm. Other ideas for a makeshift sling include:

- use the casualty's jacket by placing the hand of the injured arm inside the fastenings or by pinning the hem up to support the arm;
- use a belt, tie, scarf or a pair of tights to support an arm using a 'collar and cuff' arrangement – but don't use this method if you think the casualty's forearm is broken; and
- if you don't have a safety pin to secure a sling at the elbow, twist the point round and tuck it into the sling at the front of the arm.

How to stop an injured lower limb from moving

Often the only treatment a lower limb injury needs is to be steadied and supported until the ambulance arrives. But if there is a long way to move the casualty to the ambulance or the ambulance's journey to hospital will take a long time, the injured limb may need to be kept still by a bandage or by a bandage and splints.

TRACTION

Before an injured limb is bandaged, it may need to be straightened. Very gently pulling an injured limb straight is called 'traction' and it helps relieve pain and reduce bleeding.

When applying traction to a leg

- always explain to the casualty what you are going to do;
- make the casualty as comfortable as possible;
- straighten the injured leg gently, by supporting the injury while traction is applied at the ankle;
- to apply traction, the ankle should be pulled gently but firmly away from the knee but keeping it in line;
- gently bring the uninjured limb alongside the injured one to use it as a splint;
- keeping traction steady at the ankle, gently slide bandages into position using the natural hollows of the leg;
- ease the bandages into the required positions by sliding them backwards and forwards;
- put padding between the legs to help protect the injury and prevent rubbing at the knees and ankles;
- tie a narrow fold figure-of-eight bandage around the ankles, tying off on the edge of the shoe;
- tie a broad-fold bandage around the knees, and a narrow-fold both above and below the injury, tying all off on the uninjured side.

Handling and transport

16

Moving any casualty can be risky for both the casualty – it may make their condition worse – and for the first aider. Unless you have undertaken practical training in moving and handling, you should not try to move a casualty unless they are in immediate danger.

RISK ASSESSMENT

Before you try to move anyone or anything, you must think about the risks involved. Risks fall into four groups – the task, the load, the area and equipment, and the 'movers'. As you think about each one, ask yourself these questions.

The task
- Is the move really necessary?
- Can the casualty move themselves?
- Do you need help?
- Is there a lifting aid available?

The load
- How big and heavy is the casualty?
- What is wrong with the casualty?
- Will moving them make things worse?
- Can the casualty help you or will they hinder you?
- Are you using anything (a splint, for instance) that will make the move harder?

The area and equipment
- Are any lifting aids (a stretcher, for instance) in the right place?
- Have you made enough space for the move?
- What sort of ground will you be moving over?

You, the 'mover'
- Are you properly trained in moving and handling?
- Do you know the other people who may be helping and what they can do?
- Are your clothes and shoes suitable for lifting?

Next, decide what equipment you are going to use and how you are going to move the casualty. Moving a casualty is usually a team effort so choose a team leader who understands the moves to be made and who can give clear instructions to the rest of the team. The team members must follow the instructions.

Before you lift a casualty, all the team must understand these simple steps to safe handling.

- Think before you lift.
- Stand as close as possible to the casualty or lifting aid.
- Bend your knees.
- Keep your back straight but do not let it become rigid.
- Use your legs to provide the power for the lift.
- Move smoothly.
- Hold the casualty as close to you as possible.

MANUAL LIFTS

This sort of move puts the first aider at most risk. Unless you are assisting a walking casualty, you should only try to move a casualty by yourself in an emergency. Try to encourage the casualty to move themselves as much as possible. *Never* try to move a casualty on your own unless it is absolutely necessary.

MANUAL LIFTS ON YOUR OWN
The human crutch

- Stand on the casualty's injured side, pass their arm around your neck, and grasp their hand or wrist.
- Ask the casualty not to drag on your neck – if this is not possible, try another method of movement.
- Pass your other arm around the casualty's waist, grasping their waist band or clothing to support them.
- Move off on the inside foot, taking small steps and walking at the casualty's pace.
- A walking stick may also give the casualty more support and take some weight off you.

Cradle

This method is only suitable for small casualties, such as children.

- Squat down beside the casualty and pass one of your arms around their body above the waist.
- Pass your other arm under their thighs and hug their body towards you as you stand up.

Piggy-back

This method is also only suitable for small casualties, such as children.

- Crouch down in front of the casualty with your back towards them.
- Ask the casualty to put their arms over your shoulders and grasp their hands together.
- Hold the casualty's thighs and rise smoothly keeping your back straight.

Drag method
- Crouch down behind the casualty and help them to sit up.
- Ask the casualty to put their arms over their chest.
- Pass your arms under the casualty's armpits and grasp their wrists.
- Pull the casualty backwards as you squat-walk.
- Remember that the casualty's head and neck are unprotected.

Don't! use the drag method if the casualty is unconscious or has shoulder injuries.

MANUAL LIFTS WHEN HELP IS AVAILABLE

Two-handed seat
- This should only be used in an emergency when no other method is possible.
- Squat facing one another on either side of the casualty.
- Cross your arms behind the casualty's back and grasp their waistband.
- Pass your other arms under the casualty's knees and grasp each other's wrists. Bring your linked arms up to the middle of the casualty's thighs.
- Move in closer, straightening your backs and rise slowly moving off together.

Fore-and-aft carry
This move should only to be used to load a
casualty onto a chair or stretcher.
- Sit the casualty up and put their arms
  across their chest.
- Squat behind the casualty, and slide your
  arms under their armpits.
- Grasp the casualty's wrists firmly.
- Ask your helper to squat beside the
  casualty, pass their arms under the
  casualty's thighs and take hold of the legs.
- Working together, rise slowly.

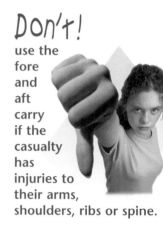

Don't!
use the
fore
and
aft
carry
if the
casualty
has
injuries to
their arms,
shoulders, ribs or spine.

MOVING AND HANDLING USING EQUIPMENT

If you intend moving a casualty using specialist equipment, you must be
properly trained to do so. If you have not been trained, you will put the
casualty and yourself at risk.

CARRY CHAIRS
When using a carry chair
- always explain to the casualty what you are going to do;
- get the chair ready, following the manufacturer's instructions;

- make sure the canvas seat and back are in good condition and not showing signs of wear and tear;
- make sure the wheels move freely and there is no sign of damage to welded joints;
- check that the safety strap is in working order;
- sit the casualty in the chair;
- always make sure someone stays behind the chair to stop it from tipping back; and
- secure the safety strap over the casualty's arms and place their feet on the footrest.

Handy hint!

Always tell the casualty what you are going to do.

How to use a carry chair on smooth ground
- Make sure the casualty is strapped in the chair.
- Tip the chair back gently and push it forward, keeping a steady speed.
- Take the corners wide to prevent overbalancing.

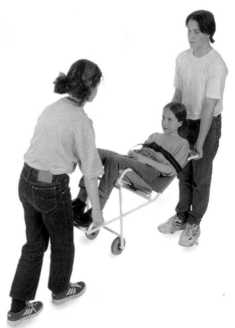

How to use a carry chair to go down stairs
- Put the chair at the top of the stairs.
- Tip the chair back, and wheel it to the edge of the stairs.
- Your helper should stand a few stairs down at a comfortable level with their back to the stairs.
- Your helper should squat down and grasp the handles on the chair's footrest.
- The two first aiders should check they are both ready then straighten their knees to lift the chair.
- Take the stairs one at a time, making sure you are keeping your balance.
- When you reach the bottom, don't put the chair down until you are both off the stairs.

How to use a carry chair to go up stairs
Reverse the procedure described above.

Handy hint!

If you need to put the carry chair down for a rest, always try to use a landing as it can be difficult trying to lift safely again on a flight of stairs.

STRETCHERS

Stretchers are used to carry casualties who are not able to walk. They come in various forms.

When using any type of stretcher
- check stretchers regularly for wear and tear and always test a stretcher before use;
- explain to your casualty what you are going to do and what the stretcher is for; and
- always use safety straps if the casualty is unconscious or if you are moving them over a long distance or rough ground.

STANDARD STRETCHER

This is known as a Furley Stretcher. It consists of a canvas or plastic sheet attached to two carrying handles with feet on the underside. The Utila Stretcher is similar to the Furley but is lighter and folds in the centre to become more compact for storage.

Handy hint!

Always make sure the hinged cross bars are locked into the open position before placing a casualty on the stretcher. Take care not to trap your fingers when collapsing the stretcher.

CANVAS-AND-POLES STRETCHER

This is used to lift a casualty from the ground onto another stretcher, particularly if there is not enough room to use a rigid stretcher. It is made up of a sheet of canvas or plastic into which poles are inserted for moving. Spreader bars are used to make the stretcher rigid. A version is also available with handles instead of carrying poles.

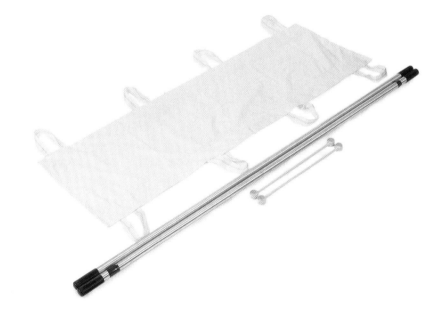

How to use a canvas and poles stretcher

- Concertina-fold one end of the canvas into the centre.
- Gently lift the patient's hips no more than 2.5 centimetres (about one inch).
- Push the canvas through the hollow in the casualty's back.
- Pull the top part of the canvas up to the casualty's head.
- Pull the bottom part of the canvas down under the casualty's feet.
- Slide the poles up the sleeves of the canvas and fit the spreaders over the ends of the poles for rigidity.

ORTHOPAEDIC STRETCHER

This light weight stretcher is also known as a 'scoop' stretcher. It lets you lift casualties with very little movement. Orthopaedic stretchers are particularly used to move casualties with major injuries such as spinal damage. The stretcher splits in two so it can be placed under the casualty then reassembled so the casualty can be lifted.

How to use an orthopaedic stretcher

- Put the stretcher alongside the casualty, adjusting it so that it is slightly longer than the casualty at each end.
- Separate the two halves of the stretcher then ease one side under the casualty, followed by the other,.
- Re-join the head end first, whilst your helper holds the foot end in place.
- Re-join the foot end, making sure the casualty's back or buttocks are not pinched.
- The casualty can now be lifted carefully onto a standard stretcher or trolley cot using the ends only.
- The scoop can then be removed gently by uncoupling and easing away.

Don't!
use a scoop
stretcher to carry
a casualty a long
distance.

RESCUE STRETCHERS

There are a several types of special rescue stretchers for removing casualties from difficult places such as cliffs and tunnels. The two most common types are the Paraguard and the Neil Robertson stretchers. They are both designed to lift casualties vertically or horizontally in awkward situations. *Rescue stretchers must only be used by people who have been properly trained to do so.*

TROLLEY COTS

Most ambulances carry stretcher trolleys or trolley cots. These are stretcher beds on wheels. The height, tilt and knee and back rest are all fully adjustable to suit the casualty's condition. They are made of lightweight tubular steel and have telescopic handles, pull bars, guard rails and safety straps.

An unloaded trolley cot weighs about 40 kilograms so it will be quite heavy with a casualty on board.

Don't! improvise aids to help move a casualty because doing so is very dangerous. Try not to lift a casualty in equipment not designed for lifting, such as a wheelchair.

PREPARING STRETCHERS

Stretchers, particularly trolley cots, are usually prepared to receive a casualty. Blankets may be used to help keep the casualty warm and to protect against bumps and jolts. A canvas carrying sheet may be placed underneath the casualty to make it easier to transfer them between stretcher, trolley cot and hospital trolley.

Using one blanket
- Put the open blanket diagonally over the stretcher so that the corners overhang.

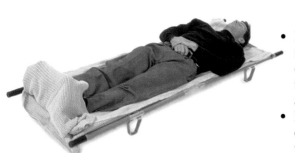

- Lay the casualty on the stretcher and bring the foot overhang over his feet, tucking it in around the ankles.
- Bring one side of the blanket over the casualty and tuck in underneath them.

- Fold the other side over and tuck it in.
- Bring the head overhang round the casualty's face and neck, making sure their face is left clear.

Using two blankets
- Put the first blanket widthways across the stretcher, covering the handles at one end.
- Fold the second blanket lengthways into three, and place on the stretcher leaving enough overhanging at the foot end to tuck round the casualty's feet.
- Fold the edges of the first blanket onto the sides of the stretcher.
- Put the casualty on the stretcher and bring the extra overhanging up over their feet and tuck it in.
- Bring one side of the blanket over and tuck it in, repeating with the other side.
- Bring the head overhang round the casualty's face and neck, making sure their face is left clear.

LOADING A STRETCHER
If possible, use the carrying sheet and poles described earlier in this chapter to load a casualty onto a stretcher. If this is not available, you can use the blanket lift or the fore-and-aft carry described earlier in this chapter.

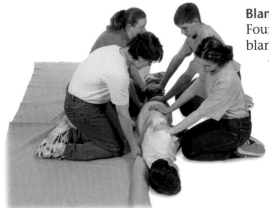

Blanket Lift
Four people are needed for a blanket lift.
- Roll a blanket lengthways to half its width and place it alongside the casualty. Gently roll the casualty onto their side and place the roll against their back.

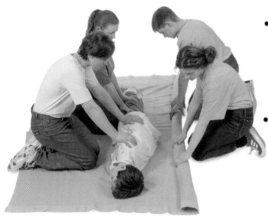

- Gently roll the casualty over the blanket roll and onto their other side, unrolling enough of the blanket on each side for the casualty to lie on.
- The carrying team should then squat each side of the casualty, two at the trunk or legs and two at the chest or head.

- Tightly roll the open blanket up against the casualty to use as handles.
- On a single command, all four helpers should lift the casualty together and transfer them to a stretcher.

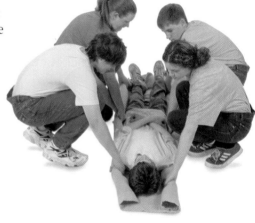

Handy hint!

The most experienced first aider should take charge and give clear commands for each action.

CARRYING A STRETCHER

Carrying a stretcher for any distance is not easy. But sometimes you may have to do so, for example if a casualty is injured during an outdoor expedition and has to be carried to the nearest road to reach an ambulance.

Always try to carry the casualty feet first, unless you are:
- carrying a casualty with serious limb injuries or hypothermia down a flight of stairs or a slope; or
- carrying a casualty with a stroke or compression in which case their head should never be lower than their feet.

To carry a stretcher
- One helper should stand at each of the four handles.
- Agree who is going to take command.
- Each helper should squat and grasp a handle.
- On a single command, the helpers should all rise together and stand holding the stretcher level.
- On a further command, the helpers should move off together, starting with the foot nearest the stretcher and taking short steps.
- To lower the casualty, the helpers should stop together then squat, lowering the stretcher until it rests gently on the ground.

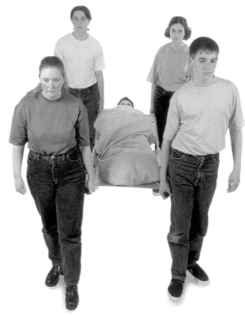

Index